Home Freezing
with Step-by-step
Pictures

Home Freezing with Step-by-step Pictures

Rena Cross

W. Foulsham & Co. Ltd
London · New York · Toronto ·
Cape Town · Sydney

W. FOULSHAM & COMPANY LIMITED,
Yeovil Road, Slough, Berkshire SL1 4JH

ISBN 0–572–01165–2

© Copyright. W. Foulsham & Co. Ltd 1982

Photoset in Great Britain by
Rowland Phototypesetting Ltd
Bury St Edmunds, Suffolk
Printed in Hong Kong

Contents

Choosing a freezer

The advantages of freezer ownership

Promoting freezer ownership is not just an attempt on the part of the manufacturers to increase sales, but stems also from a genuine conviction that it is up to each one of us to raise the quality of our lives as far as we can by our own efforts, and that the efficient use of a freezer goes a long way towards achieving this object.

There are, basically, three types of benefit available to freezer owners:

The ability to save money By buying food in bulk, by reducing transport costs incurred in frequent shopping trips, by freezing your own garden produce when it is in season, by taking full advantage of gifts of game or fish presented by friends and relatives, by freezing your left-overs thus avoiding waste, and by taking advantage of cheap buys during seasonal gluts.

The ability to save time By cooking perhaps only once a month or once a fortnight. Whenever you cook a meal that can be frozen, double your quantities and cook one to eat now, and one to go into the freezer.

The ability to choose Choosing exactly what you want to eat at any particular meal on any particular day without having to go to the shops for it, the avoidance of that particular panic when you see unexpected visitors walking up the path, or simply wanting to keep the family properly fed through any sort of domestic crisis. A freezer in the home is, above all, a liberator from what can easily become the tyranny of housekeeping.

Types of freezer owner

If we classify freezer owners for easy identification, we find that three types usually emerge.

The first type of owner buys in commercially frozen foods, rushes them home and puts them in the freezer, very, very rarely freezing any fresh foods prepared at home. In other words, the freezer is used purely as a storage cupboard. The increase in this type of freezer-ownership is shown by the increase in the sales of fridge/freezers, in which the freezer space is too small for efficient turn-over, its maximum capacity being about 22.5 kg (50 lb) of food. Such owners reduce slightly the number of shopping trips they need to make, and maintain a small variety of quickly assembled standardized meals but, owing to the high cost of commercially frozen foods, and the fact that they don't have space to freeze even their own garden produce, cannot claim more than an infinitesimal financial saving.

The second type of freezer owner probably lives in a town, has a job, may or may not have a vegetable garden, possibly takes weekend 'pick-your-own' trips into the country in season to stock the freezer, and buy farm meat and poultry. Understanding the implications of freezer-ownership, and willing to learn her own 'freezer routine', she knows all the convenience 'dodges' such as the freezing of loaves of bread, milk, and gourmet meals for special occasions. She realizes that busy people don't always feel like cooking an elaborate evening meal, but she doesn't like 'scratched-up food'. A casserole or meat pie with vegetables, followed by fruit or a pudding from the freezer takes even less trouble than eggs, chips and baked beans. This freezer owner saves money on bulk buying, especially meat, saves time and energy on busy days, and has the luxury of choice that is the prerogative of every freezer owner.

The third type of freezer owner undoubtedly gets the best value from her freezer, *as long as it is big enough*. She is probably a countrywoman, possibly a farmer's wife, with farm workers to feed as well as her family, and her freezer is likely to be of a size to contain as much as 300 kg (650 lb) of frozen food. The contents are more seasonal than those of the other two groups; she freezes virtually from the land, in quantities that ensure a steady supply of fruits and vegetables all the year round. Just as the human nutrition problems prior to the late 18th century (when cattle were slaughtered in autumn and the meat salted down for winter) were solved by the development of root crops that fed the beasts through the winter, so technology has taken a giant step forward, and the country dweller can choose, at any time of the year, exactly what food she prefers. Even if you keep your own hens, it's convenient to freeze a few eggs against the time when they're 'off lay'. When baking batches of bread, it saves time to make a double quantity of dough, and freeze half of it. If you kill a lamb or a pig, you have to deal with the whole of it without wasting any. It would last a week in the refrigerator or larder, but lasts a year in the freezer. A game shoot could yield a great deal more than one potful. Having a freezer under these conditions means making the best of the plenty around you. In addition to the saving of using her own produce or buying in the best market, there is the saving caused by not wasting. This can add up to an appreciable amount on a year-round basis. Properly used, a freezer should save its own initial cost within two years.

Types of freezer

Fridge/freezers
We have already mentioned these, and their comparatively small capacity. They will freeze only a small amount of fresh food at a time. Upright in design, they combine a freezer compartment (usually at the top) with a standard refrigerator. They take up relatively little floor space. The capacity of the freezer is about 170l (6 cu.ft.)

Upright freezers
These again take up a minimum of floor space, and have convenient shelving that makes it easy to reach in and take food packages out. They range in size from about 57l (2 cu.ft.) to 570l (20 cu.ft.). Foods approaching their storage limit, which must be used up soon, are easier to see than in the chest type of freezer, but every time you open the freezer door, warm air is admitted over the whole of the surface, however quickly you close the door again. This means that your freezer uses more power, and therefore is fractionally more expensive to run than the chest type, and will need defrosting more often. This can be minimized by opening the freezer as little as possible.

Chest-type freezers
These tend to be long, deep and narrow; in the catering trade they are often known as 'coffins'. Obviously they take up more floor space than the upright type, and need plenty of overhead space, as you not only have to lift the lid, but also have to lift it high enough to *see* what's inside, as well as reaching in to take packages out. Sizes range from about 112l (4 cu.ft.) to about 706l (25 cu.ft.). Most chest-type freezers come equipped with wire baskets and partitions, but in general the contents are not as accessible as in an upright model. On the other hand, they are cheaper to operate, as less cold air is lost when the lid is opened. Do not confuse a freezer with a conservator. Conservators can only store already frozen food, and are unsuitable for domestic use. *Note* If you are short, or have short arms, don't consider buying a chest-type freezer. You must be able to reach in and pick up packages from the floor of the freezer, and if you can't do this comfortably, it's simply not worth subjecting yourself to the annoyance of trying.

Size and location

Size
Most first-time buyers choose a freezer that is too small for them, and this is quite understandable; for when you look

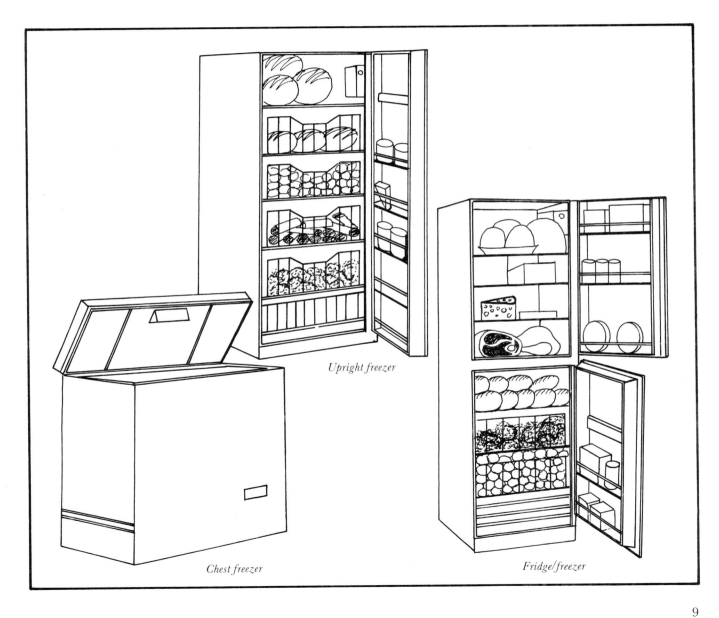

Upright freezer

Chest freezer

Fridge/freezer

at a freezer in a showroom, particularly a chest-type freezer, it looks enormous, and the idea of actually filling it seems absolutely mind-boggling. But something like 50 per cent of second-hand freezers offered for sale are being discarded because their capacity is too small, so buy a model that gives you room to have a proper seasonal turnover of frozen food.

A 112l (4 cu.ft.) freezer is a one-person freezer (and it makes good sense for a person living alone to have a freezer of this size). You can roughly estimate your family requirements by allowing 112l (4 cu.ft.) to each person. If this seems to be somewhat excessive, let's give an example. If a family of four want to eat peas once a week for a year, they will need to start off with 23 kg (50 lb) of peas, and this will take up over 28l (1 cu.ft.) of space. Of course, each time you serve peas, you reduce the amount and increase the space, but peas are only one item.

Viewed in that light, one begins to wonder whether even the 448l (16 cu.ft.) average family freezer is large enough for proper turnover, the world being so full of such a variety of freezable food! Your freezer is constantly being emptied and filled with food, the rate of movement and the type of food depending on your own life style, and it would be a pity if you were restricted by an initial choice of too small a freezer. The cost of running a slightly larger freezer is almost marginal, and in any case electricity consumption is less than most people imagine.

Location

The cost of running your freezer depends very largely on the temperature of its environment. This fact, obvious though it is, is often overlooked. If your freezer has to work hard constantly to maintain the required low temperature, it not only consumes extra electricity, but will wear out the motor quicker through sheer overwork. Ideally, then, the freezer site should be cool, but also dry, because constant damp will rust the cabinet and render the freezer totally useless.

It should be remembered that, although many freezers are almost silent in operation, most of them make some degree of noise, especially as they get older, and are subject to vibration. If you choose a hall, landing or spare room as a site for your freezer, these facts should be taken into consideration. What may seem to be almost imperceptible in daytime can be a constant sleep-wrecking irritation at night. When siting a freezer always ensure that there is a gap between the freezer and the wall, for circulation of air. Raise the freezer on blocks to prevent rusting.

If you keep your freezer in a garage or outhouse, make sure it locks, and *keep it locked*. A freezer could well hold food worth several times the cost of your freezer – nice pickings for any casual intruder.

If you have inquisitive toddlers, keeping indoor freezers locked can be a wise precaution. Small children can crawl into incredibly small spaces, and can lift heavy lids, and many freezers have automatic locks that won't open from the inside. Most modern freezers, however, are toddler-proof. If you ever throw away an old freezer or refrigerator on the rubbish dump, always strike off the lock so that under no circumstances can a child get caught inside it, and suffocate.

Anything else? Yes, if your freezer is any distance from the kitchen, have a string bag or plastic carrier to carry frozen packages in. Deep frozen food items are *not* the most cosy things to clutch to your chest, but woolly mitts are a great comfort here, too. Also, if your freezer is situated in a place not frequently visited, it is worth fitting a buzzer alarm which will warn you of any power failure to the freezer, such as a blown fuse.

Buying a freezer

I have already stressed the importance of buying as big a freezer as you can afford, or have room for. You should allow at least 112l (4 cu.ft.) of freezing space per person in the family. Chest-type freezers are normally cheaper to operate than upright freezers, but the food is normally less accessible. Consider also the location of the freezer, since chest freezers take up more floor space, although less headroom.

Ensure that your freezer has a fast-freezing facility – a control which overrides the freezer's normal thermostat and allows food to be frozen quickly. Freezers sold in the UK which bear a large star in front of three smaller stars confirm this facility. Check also that you like the operation of the freezer's controls, sliding shelves, etc. Some upright freezers have doors which can hinge from the left or the right. Your freezer should also have an interior light which comes on automatically once the door is opened or the lid is lifted. You should also enquire about after-sales service and parts availability, in case of breakdown.

When buying a freezer, don't go for the 'Free Freezer Full of Food' gimmick once so prevalent, and now fortunately a rarity. It sounded tempting when the advertisements read 'Buy a freezer, and we'll fill it with food, free', but of course the choice of food (and the quality) was the retailer's, and not yours. To save money, it is far better to deal with a discount house, or investigate special offer sales, where you can buy a freezer of reputable manufacture at an advantageous price.

Buying a second-hand freezer

Caveat Emptor, says the old proverb – Let the buyer beware! Many potential first-time freezer buyers feel that it would be a wise move to try out the freezer way of life by starting with a second-hand model, and this may indeed be so, if they take certain precautions:

a) See the freezer *in action*, and well frosted up. Listen to the motor; if it's 'labouring', it isn't working properly, and may break down at any moment.

b) Find out why it's being sold. The only really valid reason, other than emigration, is that the vendors want to buy a bigger freezer.

c) Know the difference between a freezer and a conservator. This is a trap you might well fall into if buying an ex-shop-fitting, as a conservator can look exactly like a chest-type freezer. But it's function is simply to keep already frozen food (particularly ice-cream) from defrosting. It won't freeze fresh food, and it won't always refreeze food that's started to defrost. A freezer must be able to not only keep frozen food stored at a temperature of $-18°C(0°F)$, but must also be able to lower the temperature of fresh and cooked food introduced into the freezer to $-28°C$ ($-18°F$). This is done by fast freezing.

Remember, finally, that a freezer is at its most effective when fresh produce – especially fruit and vegetables – are at their cheapest. Therefore, early summer is a good time to buy a freezer.

Using your freezer

Why freeze food?

We live in a world covered in bacteria – some harmful to us, others harmless. This is a fact of life which we all accept. All food becomes contaminated to a certain degree, and that is a fact we have to accept, too. Under certain conditions, where temperatures are high and ventilation poor, bacteria multiply rapidly, increasing the danger of food poisoning. Under normal refrigeration, bacterial growth – and food deterioration – is slowed down, and the food keeps safe for longer – for about a week where, at room temperature, it may keep only for a day, or even only a few hours.

Under the lower temperature of a freezer (−18°C/0°F), bacterial action is halted, although the bacteria are not killed off. Once the food is thawed, the bacterial action starts again, which is why once it is completely thawed, food should be used as soon as possible.

Freezing is the only method whereby food can be stored for a certain length of time without changing its flavour and nutritional value, although most fruits and some vegetables do change in texture. This is because the water, contained in all food stuffs, forms into expanded ice crystals (you will have noticed how milk in the bottle expands when frozen on your doorstep in winter and pushes its own cap off), which rupture the delicate cell walls and often cause their structure to collapse. The cell walls in meat or poultry or bakery goods are sufficiently tough to resist this ice pressure, but those of most fruits and vegetables soften and become limp. So it's no good slipping a few apples into the freezer under the impression that you can bring them out in 6 months time and find them crisp and crunchy. They won't have gone bad, but they'll be mushy. Fast freezing, done by operating the fast freezing switch (or by placing food in a special compartment), helps to reduce the size of ice crystals, since the faster the food is frozen the smaller the crystals, and hence less tissue damage.

Since certain foods stay in top condition only for a limited time, storage limits are listed on pages 18 and 19 under each separate item of food. After this time the food begins to deteriorate; it starts to lose taste, colour and texture, and will, if left, eventually go bad. For any stored food to remain in top condition, it also needs to have been properly prepared and packaged, according to the instructions in this book, before being put in the freezer.

But the freezer, however useful a piece of household equipment, is no magic box. If the quality of the food put into it does not deteriorate for some considerable time, it also does not improve. If you have bought a joint of meat that your experience tells you looks as if it were going to be tough, putting it in the freezer will not alter that. It won't toughen in the freezer, but it won't tenderize, either. Neither will fruit ripen, or vegetables improve in any way. All you are doing is suspending time in the life of the food.

Making a start

Nobody can tell you what to put in your freezer, how long to keep it there (except to advise on storage limits), or when to take it out. A manual such as this can only describe every process from buying, through preparing, packaging, labelling, freezing to subsequent thawing. 'I just can't get started,' wailed a housewife of my acquaintance, who had considered her garden immense and the amount of food it produced unmanageable until she came to try to stock her new freezer. She prepared, packaged, labelled and froze for days on end and had, it seemed to her, only filled up one corner of her chest-type freezer. 'I don't know why they talk about saving space. My problem is to *fill* it, not save it,' she complained.

However, the keenest of gardeners do not limit their freezer contents to home-grown fruit and vegetables; your freezer is a store for all kinds of other food, and the greater the quantity you buy, the greater your cash saving. One of the greatest changes in food buying trends over the last decade is the availability of bulk foods to members of the public, who now enjoy facilities previously only available to the catering trades. It is estimated that these savings can amount to between a quarter and a third of your normal food bill. Your greatest advantage will probably be buying meat in quantity. It is well worth shopping around to find a butcher who not only gives you a good discount, but may also specialize in the kind of meat that you prefer, and is willing to cut it up to your individual requirements.

In addition to the financial savings of bulk buying, and the more obvious one of freezing your own fruit and vegetables, 'pick-your-own' can represent a great saving, especially if the whole family make an expedition to the country to bring back berry fruits and vegetables. But a word of warning where pick-your-own is concerned – the prices charged do not necessarily represent a reasonable saving, or even any saving at all, if you take into consideration the work involved, and cost of petrol or bus fares. Prices may be virtually as cheap in adjacent towns, and it might be as well to check first, because most fruit picking and vegetable lifting is hard work, and fresh air and activity engenders healthy appetites, which may not be cheap to satisfy. In any case, it would be as well to compare prices at various pick-your-own locations.

A freezer is not usually an impulse buy. If it is bought on impulse – as a special bargain, either new or second-hand – it doesn't have to be put into immediate use. Certainly not in winter, when vegetables and fruit are scarce. The new freezer owner is worried by the fact that she should certainly not be starting now; she should have started last year. And with good reason, because it takes at least one run through the four seasons before you can develop properly your own freezing system, and during those four seasons you must chart down what the family liked, and what was a gastronomic disaster. It's useless for the author of any freezing manual to try to dictate what should or should not form the contents of a particular freezer, because freezer owning families come in such a variety of sizes, tastes, incomes and priorities. There is really no way of simultaneously catering on the one hand for the needs of the retired country couple whose hardest decision may be whether to eat the grouse or the pheasant first, and on the other for the household where each child demands a colossal birthday party, and the youngest tends to bring the whole of his cub pack home for an instant hamburger snack.

Your freezer only functions properly and efficiently if it is *at least three-quarters full*. Empty space wastes electricity and costs you money. When you first buy your freezer, have it delivered into its preselected position, and then wash it out with a solution of 2 tablespoonfuls of bicarbonate of soda in 4.5 litres (1 gallon) warm water. Dry thoroughly. Then switch it on, following the maker's instructions, and leave it running for a day or two until it is thoroughly cold. Taping the socket to the wall will ensure no-one inadvertently disconnects the freezer. Then, unless you live on a farm, and plan to kill fresh meat, go out and *buy*. You will, it is hoped, have considered your shopping list before you bought the freezer, and will be able to go straight to your supplier to pick up your bulkiest items: meat and poultry.

Estimating space

It is a good idea to stock your freezer first with basic items – meat, fruit and vegetables – which take advantage of seasonal price drops and general availability. Here's how to estimate how much of these items your freezer will hold.

Twenty-eight litres (1 cu.ft.) of storage space will accommodate 9.25 kg (20 lb) of meat, but this means 28l (1 cu.ft.) of *solid* meat; odd shaped joints like shoulders and legs of lamb and pork take up more space.

It would be a good idea to lay down your stocks of vegetables and fruits on the following very approximate principle. When packed in rigid cartons:

You can get 450g (1 lb) peas in a 600-ml (1-pint) carton.

You can get 450g (1 lb) green beans, or 450g (1 lb) blackberries, or 450g (1 lb) rhubarb in a 750-ml (1¼-pint) carton.

You can get 450g (1 lb) asparagus or 450g (1lb) broccoli, or 450g (1 lb) cauliflower, or 450g (1 lb) apple slices in a 1.2-litre (2-pint) carton.

You should be able to fit 35 square or rectangular rigid 600-ml (1-pint) cartons in 28l (1 cu.ft.) of space, or 30 600-ml (1-pint) round tub cartons.

When you have in your freezer what most freezer-owners would consider the basics, the inclusion of other food becomes a personal choice, with cooked and pre-pared meals (especially those made as a result of bulk cooking and chain baking) being especially useful and economical. A few loaves of bread, tubs of ice cream, etc., are also useful standbys. Over the first few months of freezer-ownership, you may find yourself involved in a quick turnover of food, using items that you have frozen long before they reach their storage limit; but the interval lengthens as you become more experienced.

Packaging for the freezer

All food placed in the freezer must be properly wrapped, not only to avoid untidiness and to keep the flavours apart, but to insulate it against 'freezer burn', which affects meat and poultry particularly, making it dry, blotchy and tasteless. Packaging must be waterproof, vapourproof and airproof, and specifically suitable for use in freezers.

There are many different types of freezing packaging available, and once you become experienced in pack-aging techniques, you will develop your own preferences. Your freezer shop will carry a wide stock of freezer packaging material, as will many of the popular larger chain stores. Among the packaging materials you need are:

a) Polythene bags of various sizes (which can be care-fully washed, dried and used again).

b) Clingfilm and other types of freezer wrap.

c) Freezer paper for outerwrapping, being mois-tureproof and greaseproof.

d) Butcher's muslin or cotton stockinette.

e) Aluminium kitchen foil.

In addition, you can make quite substantial savings by using the following, some of which are essential for pack-aging fruit, cooked meals or liquids:

a) Empty polythene and plastic snap-lid containers, such as are used for ice-cream, margarine, etc.

b) Aluminium foil dishes, pie plates and trays.

c) Rustproof aluminium tins with close-fitting lids.

d) Polystyrene trays for holding chops and other small meat goods.

e) Toughened glass jars with screw lids.

f) Waxed cartons originally used for ice-cream, yoghurt, etc.

g) A range of freezer-to-oven cookware.

You will also need special freezer labels (any others will rapidly become unreadable), chinagraph pencils or felt-tip pens, waterproof sealing tape, and paper- or plastic-covered wire twist ties.

Leaving a headspace

When packing food for freezing in rigid containers, (polythene or plastic boxes, waxed cartons, etc.), space must be left between the top of the food and the lid, to allow for expansion of moisture. This should be between 1cm (½ inch) and 2.5cm (1 inch); the more moisture the food contains, the greater the headspace needed. Narrow-topped containers need slightly more space than wide ones.

Space should also be left when packing food in polythene bags; withdraw air from the bag with a straw before it is tied.

Labelling

It is impossible to over-emphasize the importance of proper labelling. Packages, even see-through polythene bags, quickly become obscured with frost, and the contents quite unidentifiable. You simply cannot remember, as the months progress, what was put in this or that carton, or when it is due to reach its storage limit. Write on the label in chinagraph pencil or felt-tip pen. Fasten the label onto the packet with twist ties, or when labelling a flat package, cover with strips of freezer tape. Your label should tell you what the package contains, in what quantity, when it was first put into the freezer; and preferably when the storage limit is reached, thus:

14/6/81 Sliced strawberries in syrup 300ml or ½ pint S/L 14/6/82
8/12/81 Beef stew 4 servings S/L 8/6/82

Stacking your freezer

To use your freezer efficiently, you should get as much as possible into it. Many packages take up more room than they should, simply because they are such an odd shape. One can't do much about that when dealing with joints of meat, but when you have moist foods such as fruit, and particularly fruit juice or purée, soups, sauces or stock, there is an easy method, illustrated on page 36 for 'squaring off' liquid and semi-liquid foods, for easier stacking in the freezer, with a consequent saving of space.

On the other hand, it is not a good idea to have the inside of your freezer filled with square blocks which make a solid wall. A certain amount of air circulation is required and, in a normal freezer, there should be a balanced mixture of joints, round packages and cartons, as well as square shapes to ensure this.

If you are filling your freezer 'from scratch', either because it has just been defrosted or because you are filling a new freezer for the first time, don't forget to turn onto fast freeze for 4 or 5 hours before putting any food in.

Freezers have a daily freezing capacity; this is the volume of food which can be fast frozen in 24 hours. The recommended capacity for freezing over this period can be found in the maker's instruction book, or sometimes it is stamped on the sides or back of the cabinet. As a general rule, it is about 10 per cent of the freezer's total capacity.

Very small items of food, say a small pie or loaf, can be placed in an operating freezer without the need to set the fast freezing switch. This is because the higher temperature of such a small item will not affect the overall temperature of the freezer contents in the way that a greater bulk of items would.

Normally, 6 hours is long enough to freeze most items, but the following guidelines will be helpful for choosing fast freezing times for particular foods:

Type of food	Freezing time
Fruit, sliced vegetables, sliced bread, liquids, dairy produce, meat	Fast freeze for 1 hour per ½ kg (1lb) weight
Bulkier items, such as cooked dishes, whole loaves	Fast freeze for 2 hours per ½ kg (1 lb) weight

If all your items of food to be frozen do not exceed the

freezer's daily freezing capacity, they can be placed in the freezer together. Otherwise you will have to wait until one batch has been frozen before placing in the next batch. When placing items in the freezer, remember that the coldest part of the freezer is against the walls, and that the faster food freezes the better. If your freezer has a separate fast freezing compartment, then the food to be frozen should be placed in this, and removed to the main part of the freezer when frozen.

Once you start filling your freezer you should begin to enter the details of date, food, quantity, number of items and storage limit in your log book.

Keeping stock

It is a great advantage to know, at any particular time, what your freezer contains without having to half empty it to examine each separate package. This can be achieved quite easily if you keep a record or freezer log book of what you put in and what you take out of the freezer, hanging it near the freezer along with a pencil. Of course, this system only works if you make it a regular routine, and never neglect to make a note every time an item of stock in your freezer is changed. In this way you will be able to tell at a glance what items need replacing, as well as which items are nearing the end of their storage life and need to be used up.

As long as the essential information appears in your record, your choice of column headings is up to you, but below I give an example.

Many people have a freezer 'map', putting the same types of food together, for easier retrieval. A description of the type of container or packaging in your record also makes location easier.

Freezing

Packages for freezing should be placed, at least in the first instance, against the freezer wall, where it is coldest, because it is essential that the food should freeze as quickly as possible. (Most freezers have a fast freeze switch or separate fast freezing compartment). The reason that various items of food can be frozen commercially and not in a home freezer (e.g. custard tarts, meals including mashed potato, etc.) is because commercial freezers can reach a lower temperature faster.

How much food can you freeze?
The capacity of any freezer is limited, however, as it can only fast freeze about 1–2.75 kg (2–6 lb) of food per 28l (1 cu. ft.) of freezer space in 24 hours, as shown in the table below.

Type of food	Freezing rate
Fluids – gravies, soups, fruit juices, purées, fruits in syrup pack, milk and cream, etc.	1 kg (2 lb) per 28l (1 cu. ft) of freezer space in 24 hours
Solid foods – meat, fish, vegetables, bakery goods, fruits in dry pack or sugar pack, etc.	1.75 kg (4 lb) per 28l (1 cu.ft.) of freezer space in 24 hours
Dry foods – game, etc.	2.75 kg (6 lb) per 28l (1 cu.ft.) of freezer space in 24 hours

Date frozen	Food	Quantity	Number	Number packages used	Storage limit
4/3/81	Peas	450g or 1 lb	10	111	4/3/82
20/5/81	Apple purée	300ml or ½ pint	6	1	20/5/82

Making space

You must also consider the space required by the food you are going to freeze, as well as its weight, and some guidelines are given in the table on page 14. When it's coming up to the time to freeze certain items, for instance vegetables in season, it is a sound idea to begin to make space for them, possibly using this space for short-term items like bread, or cooked dishes which will be eaten quite soon.

Don't ever make the disastrous but not unheard of mistake of buying in great quantities of food for freezing, only to bring it home to an almost totally filled freezer, with no room for your purchases. This will involve you eating food from your freezer before you want to, or in extreme cases, even throwing items away.

As you put your packaged food against the wall in your freezer to freeze, enter it into your log book.

Some foods freeze better than others

Before we go on to the preparation of food for the freezer, we should consider which foods freeze well; which foods do not freeze well, and why; and which foods can't be frozen at all. And at this time, it's as well to point out that some foods represent a waste of freezer space, simply because they are available all year round. This particularly applies to such vegetables as onions; there is also hardly a season when you can't buy cabbage, but of course in either case it is worth freezing your own garden produce. It should also be pointed out that different foods, and even different types of the same food, have different storage lives.

So what can you freeze?

Meat and fish All types of raw meat, offal, poultry, game and fish (see pages 36–54).

Vegetables All vegetables; but some, such as lettuce, cabbage and celery will wilt. Tomatoes will soften and can only be used for cooking. Potatoes freeze only as chips or when very new (see pages 70–87).

Fruit All fruit except melon, which goes tough and leathery and loses flavour. All fruit, especially soft fruit (strawberries, raspberries) softens with freezing (see pages 55–69).

Bakery produce Most types of bakery produce; bread dough, bread; pastry of all types, both raw and cooked; cakes and sponges, iced or plain (see pages 88–95). The exception is macaroons, which are a freezer disaster!

Dairy produce Eggs without shells, beaten or separated; homogenized or skimmed milk; cream with over 40% butterfat content (e.g. double cream, clotted cream), single or 'top-of-the-milk' cream, with added sugar; butter; cheese, which will crumble when thawed, and can only be used for cooking. Cheese dips for short storage only. Cream cheese does not freeze well, because it separates out. Hard-boiled eggs harden and go leathery; the yolks of raw unseparated eggs harden (see pages 96–100).

Cooked foods A wide range of cooked foods, including soups, main courses, puddings and some sauces. But you should avoid the use of garlic, the flavour of which changes and becomes unpleasant within a week; and herbs, which tend to taste mouldy after about a month. (This is why the storage limit of stuffed poultry is about a month, and of unstuffed poultry about a year.) Food can be cooked with the herbs in a muslin bag, which should be removed before freezing. *The storage limit of any cooked dish is that of the ingredient with the shortest storage time.*

Note Rice and pasta There is some controversy about freezing cooked rice and pasta, although many cookery experts recommend it. My own feeling is that where either are incorporated in dishes with other foods (stuffed peppers, lasagna, etc), one can save time by cooking a double quantity and freezing one for about a month. It also makes economic sense to freeze rice and pasta leftovers, again for a strictly limited time. But this depends a great deal on how you like your rice and pasta cooked; if you prefer it just cooked, it is best to boil your rice or pasta fresh each time – they're practically 'instant' foods anyway, because they cook very quickly. Such extras as Bolognaise sauce can, of course, be prepared and cooked ahead of time, and frozen. It is the choice of such items for your freezer that contribute to your own individual freezer way of life.

Recommended storage life in the freezer (average)
(at −18°C/0°F)

Type of food	Remarks	Storage life in months	Type of food	Remarks	Storage life in months
Beef joint	uncooked	8	Pheasant, other game birds	uncooked	6
Beef steak	uncooked	6	Venison	uncooked	8
Beef sausages	uncooked	1–3			
Beef mince	uncooked	3	**Poultry**	roast (sliced/unsliced)	2
			Chicken	uncooked	12
Veal all cuts	uncooked	6	Turkey	uncooked	6
Veal mince/cubed	uncooked	3	Giblets	uncooked	2
			Duck	uncooked	6
Lamb joint	uncooked	8	Goose	uncooked	4
Lamb chops	uncooked	8			
Lamb cutlets	uncooked	6	**Meat in cooked dishes**		
			Pies		2
Pork joint	uncooked	6	Pâté		1
Pork chops	uncooked	3	Meat loaf		1
Pork sausages	uncooked	2	Casseroles, stews		1½–2
Bacon joint	unsmoked/uncooked	5 weeks	**Offal**	uncooked	3–4
Bacon joint	cooked	1			
Bacon joint	smoked, uncooked	1½	**Fish and shellfish**		
Bacon rashers	vacuum packed	4	Cod, plaice, sole, etc.		3
Bacon rashers	unsmoked	3 weeks	Salmon, mackerel, trout, herrings, etc.		2
Bacon rashers	smoked	2	Crab		1
			Lobster		1
Tongue	uncooked	3	Shrimps, prawns, shellfish (mussels, oysters)		1
Tongue	cooked	1	Fish in cooked meals		1
Game					
Rabbit, hare	uncooked	6			

Type of food	Remarks	Storage life in months	Type of food	Remarks	Storage life in months
Vegetables			**Dairy produce**		
Most vegetables (peas, beans, carrots, etc.)		12	Butter	unsalted	12
			Butter	salted	6
Artichokes		3	Margarine, lard, dripping		5
Asparagus		12	Cheese		3–6
Aubergine		12	Cream		4
Avocado pear		2	Milk	homogenised	1
Beetroot	sliced/whole	6	Eggs		6
Broccoli		12	Ice cream		1
Cabbage		6			
Cauliflower		6			
Celery		12			
Herbs		6	**Bakery produce**		
Leeks		6	Bread	unbaked brown/white	2
Mushrooms	raw	1	Bread	baked brown/white	6
Mushrooms	cooked	3	Bread rolls		1 week
Onions		3–6	Cakes	baked/undecorated	4
Peppers		12	Cakes	baked/decorated	3
Potatoes	new/baked/roast	1–3	Cake mixture	unbaked	1
Potatoes	chipped	3–6	Scones	cooked	6
Purées	varies	6–12	Biscuits	baked/unbaked	6
Root vegetables		12	Pastry	shortcrust/flaky/ puff (unbaked)	3
Spinach		12	Pastry	shortcrust/flaky puff (baked)	6
Fruit dried		1	Pies	unbaked/baked	3
Fruit purées		4–8	Flans	unfilled/unbaked	3
Fruit juice		6	Flans	filled/baked	2
Fruit in sugar or syrup pack		8–12	Puddings	steamed/baked	3
			Sandwiches		1
Fruit without sugar or syrup pack		2–12	Soufflés		3

Thawing

Food should be frozen as quickly as possible but, after being taken out of the freezer, it should be thawed as slowly as possible, preferably in a refrigerator. The thawing process is only completed when *all* frost crystals have dissolved.

Foods which do not need thawing include cooked dishes to be served hot, which can be warmed through right away, and vegetables which should be cooked until tender.

It is a common practice to cook fish without thawing it and, from a health point of view, there is nothing against this. But it does nothing for the flavour – try thawing the fish properly before cooking it, and see.

Hastening thawing

There is no proper way to hasten thawing, particularly of meat or poultry. Dropping a joint of meat into a bowl of hot water will simply seal the outside (as you do when braising), and ensure that the centre doesn't thaw out. Using warm water is fractionally less disastrous, but immersing a joint in water of any temperature, even cold, will draw out not only blood and frost crystals, but flavour as well, and you will end up with a totally tasteless meal.

However, there is a way to solve the problem. If you plan a joint for Sunday, write on the lid or door of your freezer in chinagraph pencil early in the week 'Take out topside joint on Friday', because taking it out on Friday will give it sufficient time to defrost comfortably in the refrigerator. If you feel foolish writing notes to yourself, think how you're going to feel when you serve hamburgers for Sunday lunch because you forgot to remove the meat from the freezer in time!

Remember also, small items frozen in batches thaw quicker if separated. So put clingfilm or foil between chops and hamburgers before freezing them, and you can ease them apart to hasten the thawing process.

Thawing poultry and game

Poultry and game should be thawed in the refrigerator and not at room temperature. Without being unduly alarmist, it should be remembered that table birds are a fruitful source of salmonella, and freezing does not kill off bacteria, but simply keeps them in abeyance. As thawing starts, it is advisable that the bird should be defrosted at a temperature (in the refrigerator) that discourages rapid multiplication of these bacteria, which would take place at room temperature. The bacteria are killed off by *proper* cooking, the bird being cooked right through, including the inside. This particularly applies to turkeys and geese, which take longer to thaw and a longer time to cook right through.

Almost all the bacteria found in raw meat are killed off by careful and adequate cooking. But 'spoiled' cooked meat carries potential danger, especially if eaten cold, which is why cooked meats cannot be refrozen.

Thawing fish

It has become (regrettably) an accepted practice to cook fish without thawing it first, but people who do this never really get to enjoy the proper taste of the fish.

If you are crumbing fish for frying, you'll need to defrost anyway, or the crumbs won't adhere. Oily fish should always be allowed to thaw out properly, to develop its full flavour.

Refreezing

As we have already said, thawing is only completed when all frost crystals have dissolved. When considering refreezing various types of food after partial or complete thawing, remember the advice given on page 21.

Ice cream This is possibly an exception to the rules. As many types have a great deal of air whipped into them during manufacture, it goes surprisingly thin and flat if partially thawed. If the quality justifies it, you can whip it up again before refreezing. Buy ice-cream in bulk containers from which you can easily take out portions of the 'soft-scoop' variety, without the need to let it soften. To dig out frozen-hard ice-cream, stand the scoop in a jug of boiling water for a moment or two until it's warm.

Type of food	Partly thawed	Completely thawed	Remarks
Raw meat, offal, poultry without stuffing	Refreeze	Cook and refreeze	Check smell and appearance Do not take chances
Stuffed poultry, game	Do not refreeze	Cook and use as soon as possible	Check smell and appearance. Do not take chances
Fish, shellfish	Refreeze fish, but not shellfish, which should be used at once	Use at once. Do not refreeze	Check smell and appearance. Do not take chances if doubtful about quality
Cooked meat dishes, meat pies	Do not refreeze. Eat as soon as possible, first heating through thoroughly		Check smell and appearance. Do not take chances if doubtful about quality
Fruit	Can be refrozen, but fruit, fruit juices and purées deteriorate in flavour and appearance after even partial thawing, and are better eaten at once		
Vegetables	You can refreeze all types of vegetables		
Bakery produce	Refreeze, but use as soon as possible	Do not refreeze. Use at once	
Dairy produce	Because of the very short freezer life, it is not worth refreezing dairy goods, so they should be used up as soon as possible		

Maintenance

Your normal maintenance should consist of little more than brushing away the frost that collects on the freezer door or lid, using a nylon brush or plastic scraper. Wire brushes, knives and other sharp or hard tools may damage the freezer surface. An occasional polish with silicone cream protects the outside of the freezer.

Defrosting your freezer

How often should you defrost your freezer? Not by the calendar, but as often as it needs it – normally about once a year. You should certainly defrost it when there is ½–1 cm (¼–½in) of ice on the walls. An iced-up freezer costs more to run, and its efficiency is impaired. If the lid or door fails to close properly because of ice build-up, you risk spoiling the contents of your freezer.

Obviously, the length of time it takes to defrost your freezer will depend on many factors, including its size, how heavily it is frosted up, and how quickly you work, but the operation can usually take up most of a morning. It should be noted that the instructions which follow can also apply to dealing with emergencies discussed later, since the objective is to keep your food in the frozen state for as long as possible. It is quite possible to delay thawing for 12–24 hours, depending on the efficiency of your initial wrapping and packaging.

When a defrost is imminent, don't replenish stocks. The fewer the contents of your freezer, the easier the job will be. A few days before you defrost, collect as many newspapers as you can, as well as a few old blankets, rugs, ground sheets or other insulation-type material. Proceed as follows:

1 Pile the newspapers thickly on the floor in a cool corner.
2 Put your most precious packages in the refrigerator.
3 Stack food packages from the freezer on the newspaper, checking to see that each package is undamaged. The table on page 21 will tell you what can safely be refrozen.
4 Cover the pile of packages with newspaper, and then with blankets or similar covering to give insulation.
5 If you have an electric fan, and the weather is warm, cool air will help to prevent defrosting.
6 SWITCH OFF THE POWER BEFORE STARTING DEFROSTING OPERATIONS.
7 Unless your freezer has a drainage system, work as far as possible without water (mopping out can be a messy back-breaking chore), dislodging ice in sheets by loosening it with a plastic spatula.
8 A bucket of hot water placed in the bottom of the freezer will speed the defrosting process. Replenish with more hot water as the water cools.
9 Never use any type of disinfectant in a freezer, as it will taint the food. Once all ice is removed, wash inside walls, base and inside lid with warm water containing 2 tablespoonfuls of sodium bicarbonate per 4.5 litres (1 gallon) of water.
10 Dry the inside of the freezer thoroughly, or you will give frost formation a real head-start!
11 Switch power back on, set to maximum coldness by operating fast freezing switch. After 4 to 5 hours, replace the food. Even if the freezer does not seem to you to be at maximum coldness, it is probably colder than the outside temperature. After about 6 hours, provided the food has frozen again, switch to the normal thermostat cold setting. Remember that the coldest part of the freezer is against the walls, so place your most valuable items there first.

Dealing with emergencies

No electrical appliance is totally immune from sudden failure, but a certain amount of preparedness can minimize the risk of loss should the unthinkable occur. Remember, too, that you can insure not only your freezer, but also its contents – both from ruination due to failure, and from theft. Ask your insurance company for details.

You should keep your freezer regularly defrosted and serviced, and if the arrangements made at the time of purchase do not include an emergency repair service, then you should organise such a service without delay.

The greatest fear to freezer owners is of prolonged

power cuts. They seldom last long enough to cause more than a softening of the outer layer of food, however. If this occurs, each package should be examined individually, and items unsuitable for refreezing should be used up as soon as possible. Even after 12 hours, the temperature inside the cabinet will be lower than the ambient temperature. It is also advisable to wrap the cabinet in blankets, being careful *not* to include the heat exchanger (condenser) or motor.

In extreme circumstances, it is sometimes possible to store food with a cold store company, but you should make provisional arrangements for this *before* the emergency occurs. Alternatively, you can make arrangements with a freezer-owning friend who will play host to your most precious packages on a reciprocal basis. Con-

sider, too, the possibility of hiring a portable generator and sharing it among freezer-owning friends in the event of a prolonged, general power cut. Each freezer can last for several hours without power.

Finally, in the event of a power failure, before calling the freezer engineer, the electricity board or your cold store company, check that no-one has inadvertently switched the freezer off! This advice is offered because it is the cause of more freezing panics than all other reasons put together. Also, when going away on holiday, make sure that if the freezer is left full of food, nobody switches off the electricity at the mains. The resulting mess to which you would return is quite indescribable – and your insurance company might not be all that keen on covering the loss.

Preparing food for the freezer

Meat, poultry and game

All meat, poultry and game freezes well. In fact, unless you buy your meat 'at source', the chances are that it has already been frozen at some stage between the farm and the retail butcher's counter.

The storage life of meat in the freezer (6–8 months for beef or lamb, 10–12 months for chicken, 3–6 months for pork or veal) depends largely on the amount of fat it carries, since fat has a shorter freezer life than lean meat. Always remember that the storage life of *any* food put in the freezer is that of the *shortest-lasting* component. It might be as well to reiterate here that no food placed in the freezer improves in any way, no matter how well it is packed.

If you buy ready-trussed poultry, remember to look inside for the little plastic-packed parcel of giblets. Giblets have a far shorter freezer life (2 months) than the chicken itself, and must therefore be frozen separately.

Meat should be cut into a manageable size and, if possible, de-boned to save space. Do not add stuffing since this does not freeze well. Vacuum-packed varieties of ham and bacon freeze best. Only lean mince should be frozen. Poultry and game should be washed inside and out, then dried.

Fish and shellfish

All fish and shellfish freezes well, although preparation techniques differ slightly according to the type and size of fish. You will find these techniques dealt with on pages 47–54.

Packaging, of prime importance in all foods for the freezer, is especially so in the case of fish, as a spoilt package will contaminate surrounding foods. Fish *must* be well wrapped.

Since many freezer owners have angler husbands, and have to deal with complete, and possibly large fishes, there are instructions on pages 48–51 on how to clean, scale, portion and fillet various kinds of fish. It's a useful art to learn; skill comes with practice. To keep a freshly caught fish until needed, fill a baking tin with water, drop fish in it and then place in freezer. When it is frozen into a block remove the tin. Pack the block of ice containing fish in cling foil and place in the freezer.

Preparation

Fish can be a little slimy, and is easier to prepare if it is soaked for about 20 seconds. Lean fish (haddock, cod, halibut, river fish) should be soaked in a salt solution of 25g (1 oz) salt to 600ml (1 pint) water. Oily fish (herring, mackerel, etc) should be soaked in a solution of 25g (1 oz) ascorbic acid to 600ml (1 pint) water.

Glazing is a technique for preparing small whole fish for the freezer. After soaking the fish lay it, unwrapped, in the freezer until frozen right through. Take the fish from the freezer, dip it in cold water, and put it back into the freezer. Repeat the operation until the fish is completely coated in ice, wrap in clingfilm, overwrap, label and freeze.

Thawing is made easier if you remember to lay sheets of clingfilm, foil or freezer paper before packing and freezing, between each portion, which can be separated for defrosting.

Freezing salmon

If you are lucky enough to acquire a salmon you can, of course, freeze it whole (as you can any other fish) and then serve it on some future special occasion. But the more common practice is to cut steaks from the head and tail ends, and to leave the middle portion intact to make some sumptuous dish. If in doubt, freeze whole. You can always cut a defrosted whole fish into portions.

Freezing shellfish

Although, once thoroughly cooked and cooled, shellfish can be frozen whole, they are easier to prepare when freshly cooked, and keep better once cleaned out (see page 52).

Fruit

Of all food groups, fruit in general changes more in consistency during freezing than any other. This is because its cellular structure is more delicate than that of other foods, the frost formation causing the moisture in the fruit to rupture the cell walls.

As a general guide, the juicier the fruit, the more it will soften on thawing, the exception being thick-skinned fruit like oranges and lemons, which may (but not invariably) be frozen whole with some success. Melons and bananas do not freeze well.

Although we only give directions for apples, naturally most fruits, and mixtures of fruits, can be frozen as purée or juice. In fact, this is an economical way of using up less-than-perfect fruit. Purées, half-thawed to your personally preferred texture, are every bit as good as expensive sorbets and granitas.

Over the last decade, so much fruit has been imported into this country that, with the exception of soft fruit, which does not travel well, and some stone fruits, most fruits are available all the year round. Thus the freezing of fruit has become almost exclusively the province of the home gardener or the pick-your-own enthusiast. But it makes good sense to freeze whatever is available and reasonably priced, as so often a bad year follows a good,

25

and it's nice to be able to reach into the freezer for a light fruity dessert, or a delicious substitute for ice-cream on a hot summer day.

Packaging fruit

Whichever pack you use for fruit – dry pack, sugar pack or syrup pack, fruit tends to be moist, and tends also to leak a little. If using rigid containers (the best packaging for moist foods), see that the lid is on securely, taping it if necessary. You need to leave headspace, as with most foods in rigid containers, the normal space required between the top of the food and the lid being about 1cm (½ inch) in wide containers, 2.5cm (1 inch) in narrow ones. Purée and juice should have a little more. The moister the food, the more headspace required.

Dry pack Prepare your fruit, and place it in rigid containers without the addition of any sugar or liquid. Suitable for grapes, gooseberries, rhubarb.

Sugar pack For use where fruit has plenty of juice. Use approximately 450g (1 lb) sugar to 1.5–2.25kg (3–5 lb) fruit, according to sweetness; layer sugar and fruit alternately in rigid containers. *Alternatively* mix fruit and sugar together in a bowl, then pack in rigid containers.

Syrup pack Many fruits, especially peaches and apples, discolour when exposed to the air, and in addition to treatment with ascorbic acid, are best stored in a syrup pack, which is also suitable for packing fruits with very little juice.

The strength of the syrup depends entirely on your own personal preference, and the integral sweetness of the fruit you are using. Basically, a 'heavy' syrup, known as a 50 per cent solution, is made from 450g (1 lb) sugar dissolved in 600ml (1 pint) water, heated if necessary, and chilled before being added to the fruit to be frozen. A 'medium' syrup (40 per cent solution) needs 325g (11 oz) sugar to 600ml (1 pint) water, and a 'light' syrup (10–30 per cent solution) takes 50–100g (2–4oz) sugar to 600ml (1 pint) water.

It is as well to remember that more sugar can be added to fruit after thawing, and to be conservative in choosing which strength syrup to use. The amount of sugar in the syrup has no effect on the storage life of the fruit in the freezer.

Ascorbic acid This is often used to prevent fruit from discolouring, and is available in crystalline, powder and tablet form, usually under a trade name, and in various strengths. It can be added to syrup, or sprinkled on fruit layers when using sugar pack. Lemon juice, in approximate quantities of 4 tablespoons to 450g (1 lb) fruit, can be used instead, but it may markedly change the taste of the fruit.

Use of foil in rigid packaging Fruit often floats in syrup, and will dry out if not completely covered. Crumpling a piece of foil and putting it at the top of the container will keep the fruit under the syrup, and ensures adequate headspace.

Vegetables

Most vegetables freeze well, but cell changes caused by the formation of frost crystals make such green vegetables as lettuce and cabbage wilt, toughen cucumber and soften celery. So in general we freeze vegetables to be cooked when taken from the freezer (no need to thaw first) and not those to be used in salads or sandwiches.

Unless you have your own vegetable garden, the freezing of vegetables is a matter of taking advantage of seasonal low prices or pick-your-own. It is rather a waste of freezer space to give it to the types of vegetables that are available all the year round; carrots, for instance, unless you freeze baby ones. Perhaps, in the vegetable section, the freezer also comes into its own for such short season luxuries as asparagus and mange-tout peas – a touch of class never did a freezer owner the slightest harm!

The freezing of potatoes is not recommended, except as chips (see page 82) and the very short storage (1 month), of very tiny cooked new potatoes. When freezing cooked dishes, it is as well to omit potato, which tends to go gluey. If they are frozen successfully commercially (which is debatable), it is because commercial freezing is faster and reaches a far lower temperature.

Onions do not represent a very good freezing proposition, especially as, unless they are exceptionally well packed, they may spread their influence to neighbouring packages.

Blanching

All vegetables contain enzymes, which cause discoloration and eventual deterioration, and their action has to be halted before they are frozen. This is done quite simply, by immersing the prepared vegetables in boiling water for a few minutes, the exact times being given later on. A chip pan with a fitting wire basket is ideal for the job, although putting the vegetables in a muslin bag and immersing it in the boiling water for the required time is quite adequate. The vegetables must be then completely cooled – immediately plunge the wire basket or muslin bag into icy cold water or use really cold running water, drain well – before packing for freezing in rigid containers or polythene bags.

Bakery produce

This food group, more than any other, exemplifies the wisdom of the 'prepare-one-for-now-one-for-the-freezer' technique, because it really isn't any more trouble to make a double quantity of bread dough or pastry, or to bake two or more cakes instead of one. Baking day takes on a new meaning when it ensures that you'll have an adequately filled freezer against the day when unexpected visitors arrive. (Ten minutes in a hot oven thaws out a cake – without icing, of course. About 60 seconds flat for scones and little cakes.) About the only cakes that won't freeze are macaroons.

Convenience

It's marvellous, too, to know that you can ice a birthday cake *before* the day, when you have a little leisure, and leave it safely in the freezer – there never seems to be enough time to deal with family birthday cakes the day before the actual party. Sandwiches can be frozen, too, and not only for parties, but for picnics and packed lunches. (Remember not to include lettuce or celery, which will wilt, or hard-boiled eggs, which go tough.)

I rate very highly the convenience of being able to keep a loaf or two of bread, even if the storage limit is low (2–6 weeks). Families tend to get rather cross about bread shortages, and it's not always convenient to make a shopping trip. Loaves and rolls with crisp crust (French, Vienna, etc.), tend to soften rather quickly, after 3 days, so normal soft-crust bread, commercially baked or home-made, are a better proposition.

If making pies, tarts or sausage rolls, etc., with frozen pastry, thaw until pliable enough to use. When using frozen fruit or meat filling, thaw until the filling is pliable enough to spread neatly and evenly, and remember to allow extra baking time – about half as much again as your normal baking time.

Dairy produce

Unless you own your own cow or goat, your freezing of milk and milk products, as with the freezing of bread, is simply a domestic convenience. Frozen milk, for drinking and cooking, is vastly superior to the powdered or canned varieties. (If your frozen milk or cream separates out, whip it vigorously with a beater.) Whole goats' milk freezes very well, and has a longer storage limit (3 months) than cows' milk. Butter that has never been softened freezes perfectly well, keeping for 3–6 months according to whether it is salted or not.

Eggs

Don't try to freeze eggs in their shells; an egg-shell is nature's perfect packaging, but not designed to withstand the expansion of liquids which occur with freezing. The egg shell will break. If you have your own hens, you may consider it worth your while to freeze either the whole egg mixture, or whites or yolks only, while your hens are in top lay, to off-set the leaner days. But the freezing of whites only comes into its own when you've been making egg custard or mayonnaise, and yolks when you've made meringues, or lemon meringue pie. In fact, since we all know that egg custards and mayonnaise are the better for being made from yolks only, and that nobody ever tried to make meringues with anything but whites, the ability to freeze and store the unused part of the egg makes for better cooking, and more choice without waste.

Cheese

It can't be said that cheese freezes terribly well. It thaws crumbly, leaving it only really fit for cooking. But since cheese is difficult to store for any length of time anyway – it 'sweats', dries up, or goes mouldy – an excess of cheese does as well in the freezer as anywhere else. And it will keep for 3 months, which is better than in the refrigerator or under a china cheese cover!

Cheese dips freeze quite well, but only for 2 months. Their moisture keeps them in good condition. It's useful to be able to make your dips some time ahead of a party, but do remember to leave enough time to thaw them out properly.

Cooked and prepared meals

One of the greatest conveniences your freezer can offer you is the ability to reach inside for a previously cooked meal which can be heated through and served literally in a few minutes, having done your cooking well in advance at a more convenient time.

When cooking for the freezer, cool food as rapidly as possible, then freeze as soon as it is thoroughly cooled. When thawing and heating again, use as soon as it is ready.

Casseroles and stews

On page 101 there are directions for the freezing of casseroles and stews in convenient meal-sized portions (portioning is the key to successful use of your freezer), and for meat pies. Further to these, the following suggestions may be useful:
a) Herbs develop a mouldy taste rather rapidly. Cook herbs in a muslin bag; remove it before freezing.
b) Don't add potatoes. They don't freeze at all well, except as chips or when very new.
c) All seasonings lose a certain amount of flavour. Adjust the seasoning after thawing.
d) If you have frozen a casserole in an oven-to-freezer dish make sure that, when warmed through before serving, it really is thawed all the way through. It is quite possible to have a bubbling casserole with an icy core.

Soups and sauces

Many cream soups and sauces can be frozen successfully (see recipes on pages 105–106). On thawing, heat slowly, as they tend to separate, in which case, whisk as they warm through.

All types of soup and stock can be frozen, and if you are freezing them in polythene bags, you may find that they end up an odd and awkward shape, taking up more valuable freezer space than you feel is justified. On page

36 we illustrate a technique for 'squaring off' a polythene bag full of liquid by initially placing the bag in a conveniently shaped carton and freezing it. The carton is then removed, and you have a handy-shaped block that will stack neatly with similar blocks in your freezer.

Pies
When cooking pies for the freezer, use your usual recipe, but do not cut vents in the crust, or the filling will dry up while in the freezer. Pies are best baked in foil pie plates or dishes, as they can go into the freezer with the pie in it, taking up little space and keeping the pie edges from being broken. If you use a pie-dish or plate (which will have to be in oven-to-freezer ware), you will either be denied the use of it while it is in the freezer – and taking up extra space – or you will have to go through the operation of taking a highly breakable pie out of the plate and wrapping it for freezing, where it will remain vulnerable for the whole of its freezer life.

Boiled and steamed puddings and sponges
These freeze very well. Grease the basin well so that the pudding can be taken out for packaging and freezing.

All types of 'cake puddings'
Baked sponges, gingerbread, etc; all freeze well.

Pancakes
Freeze well.

Mousses
Freeze well.

Ice Creams
All types of ice-cream, sorbets and granitas are, of course, the freezer owner's standby.

On the debit side, jellies and gelatine desserts in general do not freeze particularly well, as they 'sweat' during freezing.

Desserts for entertaining
A number of fancy desserts can be frozen with varying degrees of success – there are recipes for some of them on pages 114 and 115. This can be a great help when you want to cook ahead fairly elaborately, perhaps for a party. Such desserts are better decorated when they are taken out of the freezer, because cream does tend to separate.

But always remember that, in addition to the type of pudding listed above, your freezer is very likely to contain a variety of fruits and fruit purées, cream, ice-cream, frozen pastry and other good things. It only needs a little time and imagination to get together a series of delicious desserts, and often the 'spur of the moment' ideas are more successful than those carefully thought out.

Rice and pasta
These are really convenience foods, since they take little time to cook and waste valuable freezer space. However, they can be frozen when an integral part of a meal.

Bulk cooking
A convenient 'half-way house' between the freezing of raw food on the one hand, and of cooked and completed meals on the other, is the technique of bulk cooking. This means cooking such standbys as beef or pork chunks, beef mince and chopped chicken before freezing. It is economical as well as convenient, when you have purchased a number of chickens from which you have planned to freeze the joints only, to use the many scrappy pieces of chicken which are left over.

Remember the inhibitions with regard to the use of seasoning and herbs (see page 28), and even if you cook in enormous quantities, pack in handy meal-sized portions.

Listed below are a few of the dishes you can quickly make from bulk-cooked meat.

Beef (cooked chunks)
Beef stew
Curry
Kebabs
Boeuf Bourguignonne
Carbonade of beef
Goulash

Spiced beef ragout
(cooked mince)
Shepherds pie
Spaghetti Bolognaise
Double crust meat pie
Savoury mince on toast, or with vegetables.

Pork (cooked chunks)
With baked or broad beans
Pork and egg pie
Sweet and sour pork
Pork chow mein or chop suey

Chicken (cooked chopped)
Quick casserole or pie
Chop suey or chow mein
Curry
Fricassee or à la king
Vol au vents
Chicken salad or sandwiches

Chain baking

Bread dough
We have emphasized already the advisability of packing various foods, including bread dough, in easily dealt-with amounts, but it is possible to thaw out more dough than you need for your bread requirements. Although dough cannot be refrozen, you can refreeze the resulting bread, buns or lardy cake, etc., even if only for a month.

If you like pizzas, this would be the time to bake the bases, which can then be refrozen, either as they are, or with the topping of your choice. It is often difficult to buy a pizza *exactly* as you like it, and as it represents a very useful quick snack, this is one of the ways to make use of the convenience of a freezer.

Pastry
Like bread dough, pastry cannot be refrozen in its raw state, but the resulting pies and tarts can be housed in the freezer. Even if you have no fillings available at that exact moment, you can 'blind' bake flans and tarts. Remember that it takes very little more time to put together frozen pastry and frozen filling to make a pie than to defrost and bake one already put together, and it allows you to choose your filling. Blind flans are also useful when making uncooked fillings for pies, of the American cream pie type, or cheese-cake.

Glossary of terms

Ascorbic acid: Substance which helps prevent fruit from discolouring. Can be added to syrup, or sprinkled on fruit layers in a sugar pack. Use ¼ teaspoonful per 600 ml (1 pint) water.

Batch cooking: Cooking food in large quantities with a subsequent saving on time and fuel. Meals so prepared can be divided into individual portions for freezing.

Blanching: Method of arresting enzyme action which would cause vegetables to lose flavour and nutritional value in storage, by first immersing them in boiling water.

Bulk buying: Purchasing food in large quantities with a subsequent saving on time and price. Allows freezer owner to buy food in its cheapest season. Many butchers sell specially prepared freezer meat packs for bulk purchase.

Chest freezer: Large capacity freezer with a lid which hinges from the top.

Compressor: One of the components of the freezer's mechanical system; usually a sealed unit with a 5-year guarantee.

Condenser: System of tubes which transfers heat from the freezer to the outside.

Conservator: Cold-storage cabinet for storing already frozen foods. It cannot freeze fresh foods.

Defrosting: Process whereby ice or frost which has formed on the walls and shelves of a freezer is removed, in order to keep the freezer operating economically and efficiently.

Dehydration: Loss of moisture from stored frozen food due to faulty packaging.

Dry pack: Method of packaging fruit without the additon of sugar or liquid.

Evaporator: System of coils which absorbs the heat from frozen food.

Fast freezing: Method whereby the temperature of fresh food introduced into the freezer is rapidly lowered.

Fast freezing switch: Manual switch which overrides the freezer's normal thermostat, to allow fast freezing to occur.

Freezer bag: Heavy quality polythene bag specifically designed for freezer use.

Freezer burn: Grey-white patches seen usually on surface of meat which has become exposed to air – and dehydrated – through inadequate packaging.

Freezer paper: Non-stick, siliconised paper designed for wrapping food for the freezer. Also known as freezer wrap.

Freezer wrap: Heavy quality clingfilm specifically designed for freezer use.

Fridge/freezer: Combination unit of freezer and standard refrigerator.

Frost: Frozen moisture which forms on the walls, shelves and packaged food inside a freezer.

Headspace: Air space left between the lid of a rigid container and the food it contains; to allow for expansion on freezing.

Loose pack: Method of freezing whereby food items are frozen before they are wrapped, so that the food is not frozen in a solid mass. Also known as open freezing.

Open freezing: See Loose pack.

Oxidation: Undesirable process in which oxygen is absorbed into frozen food. Prevented by correct wrapping and the removal of air.

Overwrapping: Method of wrapping food for extra protection against cross odours, freezer burn, etc., by wrapping first in, say, cling-film, and then in, say, aluminium foil.

Purée: Pulped or liquidized fruit or vegetables.

Rigid container: Container with screw-on or snap-on lid which requires no further sealing.

Star symbols: System of denoting the capacity of a refrigerator to store commercially frozen food, or the capacity of a freezer to freeze and then store food.

Sugar pack: Method of packaging fruit in rigid containers with added sugar.

Syrup pack: Method of packaging fruit by storing in rigid containers with added syrup, made by dissolving sugar in water.

Thawing: Process of raising the temperature of frozen food.

Thermostat: Electrical device which regulates the temperature by automatically switching on the motor when the temperature rises, and switching it off when the correct temperature is reached.

Upright freezer: Type of freezer with a door which hinges from left or right.

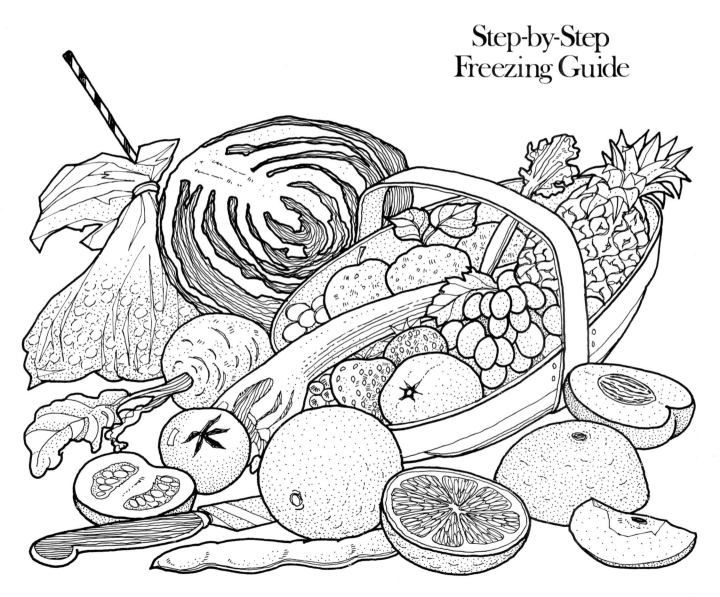

Step-by-Step
Freezing Guide

Square pack

1 Use freezer paper large enough to overlap all edges by about 7.5cm (3 inches). Draw edges together at top.
2 Fold edges over until they lie tight to the contents.
3 Taper the ends and fold them against the rest of the paper. Seal well.

Round pack

Use freezer paper, put food in one corner, and lift paper in that corner.

Fold two side pieces across top.

Roll package over, up to the end of the paper.

Fasten with tape, and label before freezing.

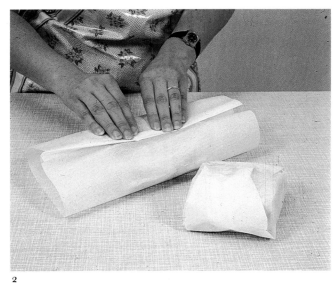

2

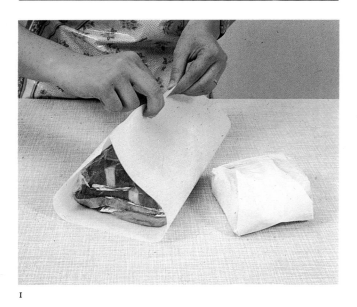

1

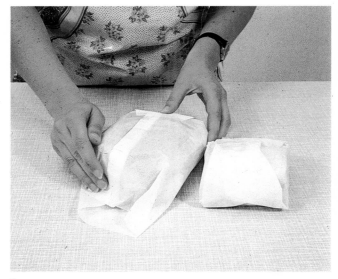

3

MEAT

Squaring-off polythene bags (this page)
1 Place polythene bag of food in square container or carton. Freeze.
2 When frozen, remove from container and return to freezer.

2

Joints (on the bone) (page 37)
1 Trim off surplus fat. Pad and wrap bones in foil to prevent package damage in freezer.
2 Cover joint with butcher's muslin or stockinette.
3 Place in polythene bag. Withdraw all possible air with a straw. Fasten bag with twist tie.
4 Always label all packages placed in the freezer, using felt-tipped pen or chinagraph pencil. Remember to record your storage limit date.

Storage limit		Thawing	
Beef	8 months	*Refrigerator*	
Lamb	8 months	8–10 hours per 450g	
Veal	6 months	(1 lb)	
Pork	6 months	*Room temperature*	
		2 hours per 450g (1 lb)	

1

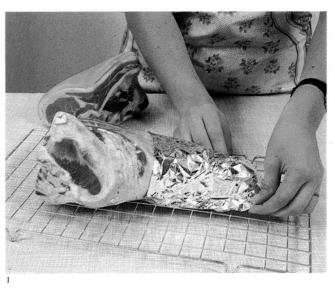

1

2

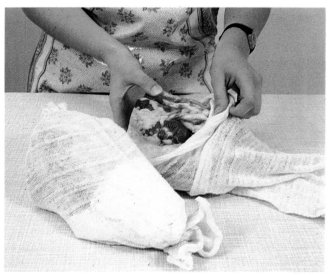

3

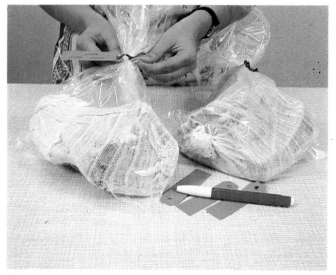

4

Joints (boneless)

1 Trim off surplus fat, wrap as for joints on the bone, or in clingfilm.
2 Outer-wrap in stockinette; tie the package securely. If air penetrates, the contents will spoil, and may contaminate the rest of the freezer contents.
3 Label and freeze.

Storage limit		Thawing
Beef	8 months	*Refrigerator*
Lamb	8 months	8–10 hours per 450g
Veal	6 months	(1 lb)
Pork	6 months	*Room temperature*
		2 hours per 450g (1 lb)

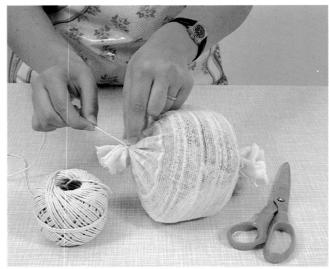

2

1

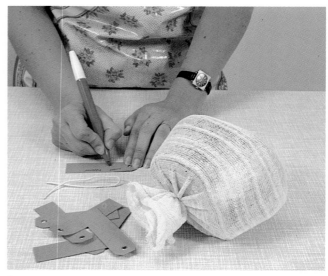

3

Steaks and chops

1 Trim and wipe. Pack in meal-sized numbers, as raw meat cannot be refrozen. Put a foil 'divider' between each chop or steak. Separated for cooking, they will defrost much quicker.

2 Wrap in clingfilm.

3 Overwrap with freezer paper. Seal, label and freeze. Adequate labelling is important as frost build-up quickly obscures the meat, making it unidentifiable.

Storage limit		Thawing
Beef	6 months	*Refrigerator*
Lamb	8 months	8–10 hours per 450g
Veal	6 months	(1 lb)
Pork	3 months	*Room temperature*
		2–4 hours per 450g
		(1 lb) according to thickness.

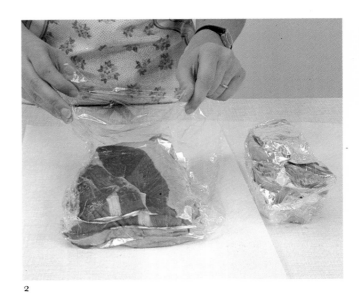

2

1

3

Mince

1 Freeze in meal-sized portions. Mince for freezing should be as lean as possible, as a high fat content cuts down the freezer life.

2 Wrap in clingfilm, then overwrap in freezer paper to make a neat secure parcel. Seal, label and freeze. Mince can be cooked before freezing, if preferred.

Storage limit	Thawing
Raw	*Refrigerator*
3 months	8–10 hours per 450g
Cooked	(1 lb)
3 months	

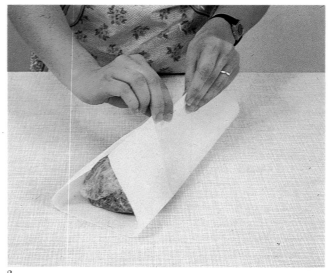

2

Hamburgers

Hamburgers should not be salted before freezing, as this cuts down freezer life. Pack as for steaks and chops, with foil 'dividers'.

Wrap with clingfilm, then overwrap with freezer paper. Seal, label and freeze.

Storage limit	Thawing
3 months	*Refrigerator*
	6 hours per 450g (1 lb)
	Or cooked directly from freezer.

1

40

Hamburgers

1

Offal (liver, heart, kidney, tongue, tripe, etc.)

1 Soak in cold water for 30 minutes. Remove blood vessels. Dry. Offal is more easily sliced when frozen.
2 Place family-sized meal portions in polythene bags, extracting air, or on polystyrene trays covered with clingfilm.
3 Tie or seal, label and freeze.

Storage limit	**Thawing**
3–4 months	*Refrigerator*
	8–9 hours per 450g
	(1 lb)
	Room temperature
	2 hours per 450g (1 lb)

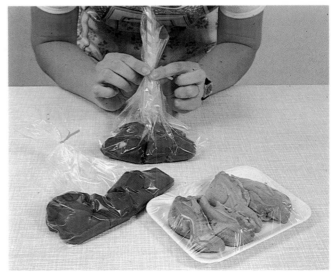

2

POULTRY

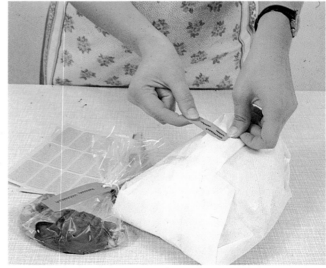

3

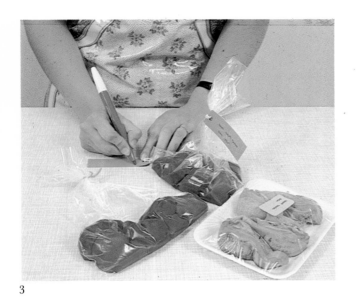

1

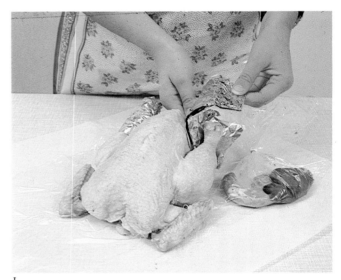

2

Chickens, ducks, geese, turkeys

1 Poultry should be plucked, drawn and trussed before wrapping for the freezer. Remove head, wing tips and feet. Wrap protruding bones in foil.
2 Wrap in clingfilm. Overwrap in freezer paper or place in polythene bag, withdrawing air.
3 Seal, label and freeze. Freeze giblets separately.

Storage limit	Thawing
(Unstuffed)	*Refrigerator*
Chickens, turkeys	*Under 1.75kg (4 lb)*
12 months	12–16 hours
Ducks, geese	*1.75–8kg (4–14 lb)*
6 months	1–2 days
Stuffed poultry	*Over 8kg (14 lb)*
1 month	2–3 days
	Thaw in the refrigerator, not at room temperature.

Poultry joints

1 Foil or polystyrene trays are ideal as a packing base for poultry joints, in one-meal quantities.
   After covering the trays containing joints with clingfilm, label and freeze.

2 Alternatively, you can complete your packing by over-wrapping in foil, with a foil lid, freezer paper or by placing the wrapped trays containing joints in a polythene bag, withdrawing air.

3 Seal or tie, label and freeze.

Storage limit
As for whole birds

Thawing
Refrigerator
5–6 hours per 450g
(1 lb)
Thaw in the refrigerator not at room temperature.

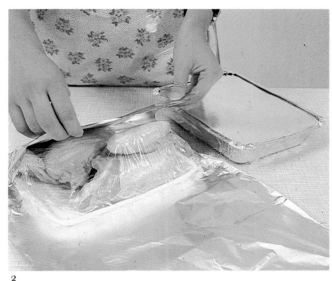

2

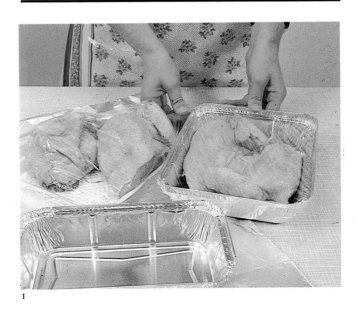

1

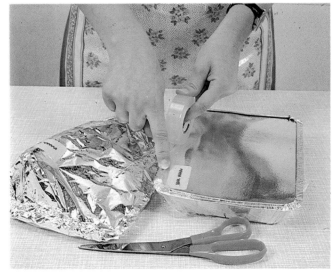

3

GAME

(Pheasant, partridge, etc.)

1 The length of time that game is hung before freezing depends on your own particular taste and the prevailing weather, usually 4–7 days in warm weather, 10 days in cool. Game must be drawn and cleaned before hanging.
2 Plucked and ready, game can be packaged as for poultry. Wrap protruding bones in foil.
3 Wrap in clingfilm.
4 Overwrap with freezer paper or place in a polythene bag, withdrawing air.

5 State on the label the number of days the game has hung before freezing. Defrosting counts as an extra hanging day.

Storage limit	**Thawing**
6–8 months	*Refrigerator*
	5–6 hours per 450g
	(1 lb).
	Thaw in the refrigerator
	not at room temperature.

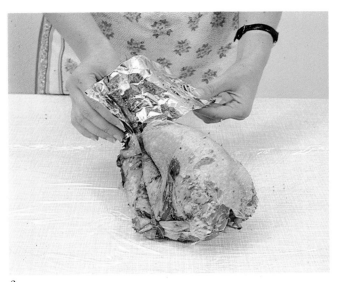

2

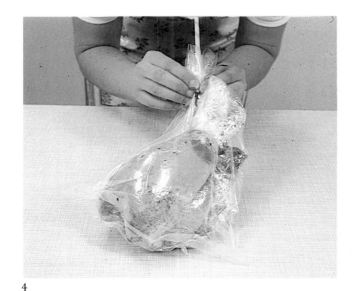

4

3

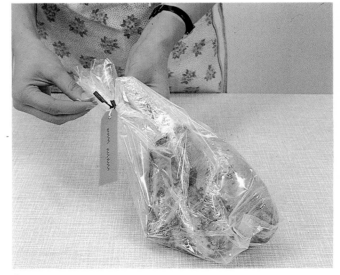

5

45

Hare

1 Cleaned and skinned, the hare can be jointed for easy packaging.
2 Foil dishes are ideal for the purpose. Wrap well in clingfilm.
3 Position foil lid.
4 Overwrap in freezer paper or place in a polythene bag, withdrawing air. Seal or tie, label and freeze.

Storage limit	**Thawing**
6–8 months	*Refrigerator*
	5–6 hours per 450g
	(1 lb).
	Thaw in the refrigerator
	not at room temperature.

2

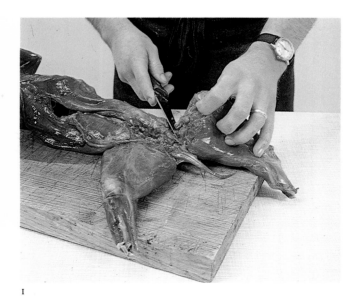

1

3

1

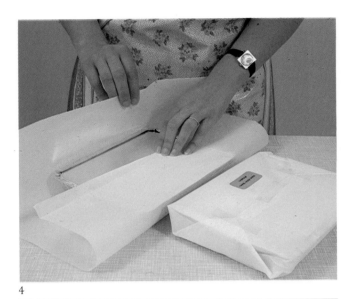

4

Fish (whole)

1 Prepare fish by cleaning and scaling. Remove head, tail and fins, if necessary.
2 *White fish* (haddock, cod, halibut, river fish, etc.). Soak in salt solution – 25g (1 oz) salt to 600ml (1 pint) water for about 20 seconds. *Oily fish* (sole, herring, mackerel, etc.) – substitute ascorbic acid for salt.
3 Small whole fish should be glazed by being laid, unwrapped, in the freezer until frozen, then dipped quickly into cold water and frozen again. Repeat until fish is coated in ice.
4 Separate with foil and wrap in clingfilm. Overwrap well with foil.
5 Seal, label and freeze.

Storage limit		Thawing
White fish	3 months	*Refrigerator*
Oily fish	2 months	6–10 hours per 450g (1 lb)
		Room temperature
		3–5 hours per 450g (1 lb)

2

Pictures 3, 4, 5, see over page

3

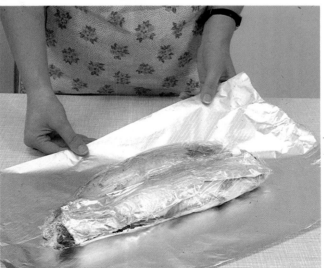

4

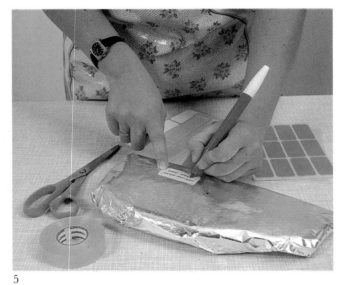

5

Fish (portioned)

1 Prepare as for whole fish, but do not glaze.

Fillets

2 Lay the fish, skin side down, on a board, cut downwards and outwards, first on one side of the backbone and then on the other, removing backbone. Trim fillets, remove skin by inserting knife at the tail, and pulling up the skin. Move knife along as skin lifts, without cutting either fish or skin.

Steaks

3 Cut prepared fish downwards in thick slices with a sharp knife, between the vertebrae, which can be felt from the inside of the fish.

4 When packing portioned fish, layer foil or clingfilm between each portion, before wrapping the whole package in clingfilm. Overwrap with foil.

Note While all food for the freezer must be adequately wrapped, foods such as fish must obviously be packed with extra care, as they could contaminate other foods. Seal well before labelling and freezing.

Storage limit
3 months
Thawing
Refrigerator
6–10 hours per 450g
(1 lb)
Room temperature
3–5 hours per 450g
(1 lb)

Lean fish can be cooked without thawing (increase cooking time by half) but if you plan to crumb your fish, thaw first or the crumbs won't adhere.

2

1

3

Picture 4, see over page

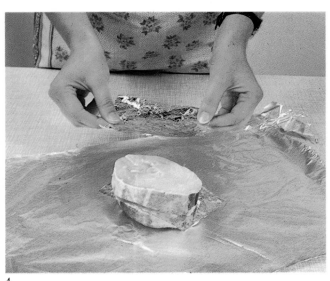

4

Salmon (whole)

1 Cut off gills and fins, clean and scale.
2 Wrap in clingfilm, then overwrap with foil. Turn over and pinch the foil edges to make a secure seal. Seal, label and freeze.

Storage limit	Thawing
3 months	*Refrigerator* 6–10 hours per 450g (1 lb) *Room temperature* 3–5 hours per 450g (1 lb)

1

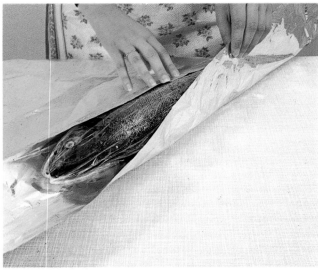

2

Salmon steaks

1 Cut prepared salmon into 2.5cm (1 inch) steaks from the head and tail. Cut the middle portion into steaks or leave whole to serve on a special occasion.
2 Layer foil or clingfilm between steaks.
3 Wrap them in clingfilm.
4 Overwrap with foil or freezer paper.
5 Seal, label and freeze.

Storage limit 2 months
Thawing
Refrigerator
6–10 hours per 450g (1 lb)
Room temperature
3–5 hours per 450g (1 lb)

2

1

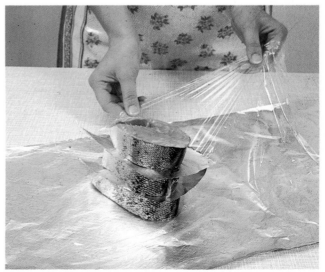

3

Pictures 4 and 5, see over page

51

4

Lobsters and crabs

1 Divide the lobster tail shell along the centre line.

2 Clean out brains and intestines.

3 Crack claws carefully to avoid injuring the flesh, nicking the shell with a heavy sharp knife on both edges. Crack by hitting the shell with the *handle* of the knife.

4 Pack in rigid containers, leaving 1cm (½ inch) headspace. Or in polythene bags, withdrawing air.

5 Seal or tie, label and freeze.

Storage limit	**Thawing**
1 month	*Refrigerator*
	10–12 hours per 450g (1 lb)
	Room temperature
	3 hours per 450g (1 lb)

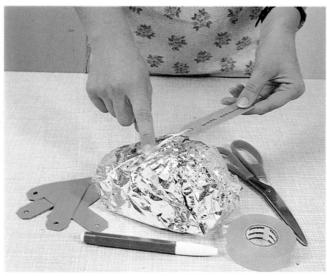

5

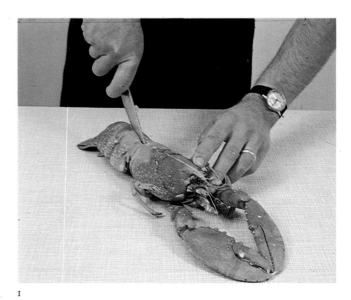

1

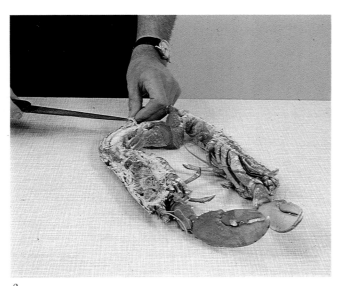

2

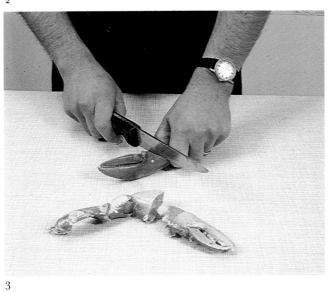

3

4

5

Oysters and scallops

1 Remove from shells, reserving juice. Wash in cold water, drain well.
2 Pack in rigid containers, adding juice, and leaving 2.5cm (1 inch) headspace.
3 Seal, label and freeze.

Storage limit	Thawing
1 month	*Refrigerator*
	8 hours per 450g
	(1 lb)
	Room temperature
	4–6 hours per 450g
	(1 lb)

2

1

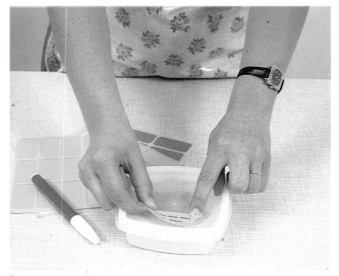

3

Apples, juice

1 Cut up and mince apples.
2 Wrap pulp loosely in muslin. Over a large bowl, press between two boards.
3 Strain juice, sweeten if required.
4 Pack in rigid containers, leaving 2cm (¾ inch) head-space.

Storage limit	Thawing
4–6 months	*Room temperature* About 2 hours per 600ml (1 pint)

2

1

3

Picture 4, see over page

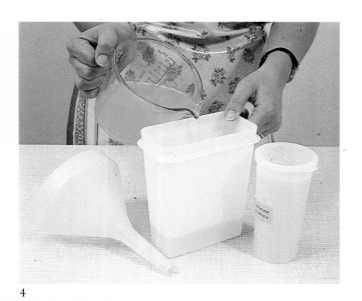

4

1

2

Apples, purée

1 Wash and cut up apples; no need to peel or core.
2 Cook until soft; sweeten if preferred. Sieve carefully.
3 Pack in rigid containers or polythene bags, withdrawing air. Seal or tie, label stating whether sugar has been added.

Storage limit	**Thawing**
6 months	*Refrigerator*
	6–8 hours per 300ml
	(½ pint)
	Room temperature
	2–4 hours per 300 ml
	(½ pint)
	If to be heated, no thawing required.

3

Apples, rings

1 Wash, peel and core apples. Cut into rings. Left-over pieces can be used when making purée.

2 Apple rings are best 'sugar-packed', i.e. alternately layering apple rings and sugar, using 450g (1 lb) sugar to 1.5–2.25kg (3–5 lb) fruit. Pack in rigid containers, leaving 1cm (½ inch) headspace.

3 Seal, label and freeze.

Storage limit	**Thawing**
12 months	If to be heated, no thawing necessary.

1

2

Picture 3, see over page

3

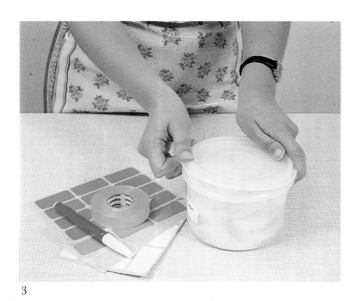

1

2

Grapefruit

1 Peel grapefruit and remove pith.

2 Either divide into segments or slices.

3 Using rigid containers, pack in 40% sugar syrup (page 26) with ½ teaspoon ascorbic acid powder added; leaving 1cm (½ inch) headspace.

4 Seal, label and freeze.

Storage limit	Thawing
12 months	*Refrigerator*
	6–8 hours per 450g
	(1 lb)
	Room temperature
	2–4 hours per 450g
	(1 lb)

3

Grapes

1 Grapes freeze well if halved and seeded.
2 Dry pack in rigid containers, or cover with 40% sugar syrup (page 26).
3 Place crumpled foil on top of the fruit to prevent it rising above the syrup. Seal, label and freeze.

Storage limit	Thawing
12 months	*Refrigerator* 6–8 hours per 225g (8oz) *Room temperature* 2–4 hours per 225g (8oz)

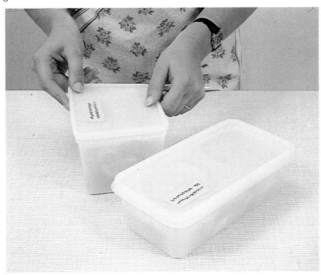

4

1

Pictures 2 and 3, see over page

2

Lemons

1 Best frozen as juice. Simply squeeze lemons, and pour juice into ice-cube trays.

2 Freeze juice in trays, then pack frozen cubes into polythene bag.

3 Withdraw air from the bag before sealing. Tie, label and freeze.

Storage limit	Thawing
12 months	*Room temperature*
	About 2 hours per 600ml
	(1 pint)

3

1

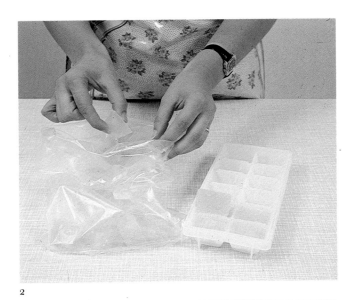

2

Pineapple

1 Choose firm ripe pineapples without any soft spots. Pare off rough outer skin.
2 Remove 'eyes' and core, saving any juice.
3 Slice, dice or cut into sticks.
4 Pack in rigid containers in 30% syrup (page 26), using juice as part of the liquid.
5 Add crumpled foil to prevent fruit rising above syrup. Seal, label and freeze.

Storage limit	Thawing
12 months	*Refrigerator*
	6–8 hours per 225g
	(8oz)
	Room temperature
	2–4 hours per 225g
	(8oz)

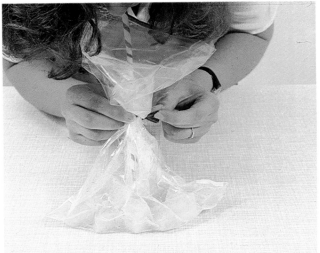

3

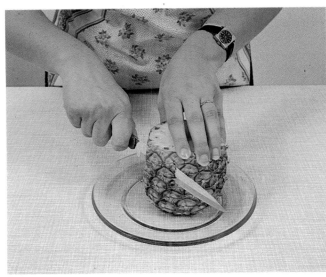

1

Pictures 2 to 5, see over page

2

4

3

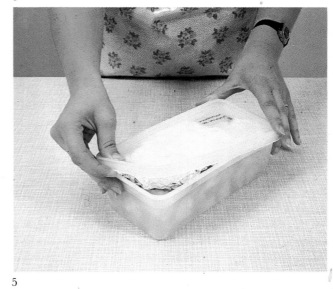

5

Rhubarb

1. Choose young but well-coloured stalks. Trim, wash and cut as required.
2. Blanch rhubarb in boiling water for 1 minute. Cool in iced water and drain well.
3. Dry pack in rigid containers, or in 40% syrup (see page 26), topped with crumpled foil.
4. Seal, label and freeze.

Storage limit	Thawing
12 months	Unnecessary. Cook until tender.

2

1

3

Picture 4, see over page

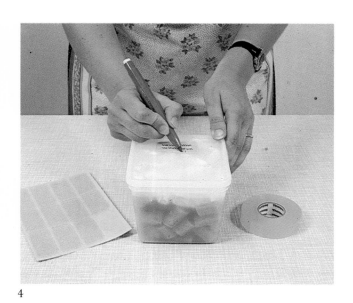

4

1

Soft fruit (gooseberries, currants)

1 Pick over fruit carefully, discarding any that are over-
   or under-ripe. 'Top and tail', wash and drain.
2 Pack in rigid containers, using sugar pack. (see page
   26). Seal, label and freeze.

Storage limit	Thawing
12 months	*Refrigerator* 6–8 hours per 225g (8oz) *Room temperature* 2–4 hours per 225g (8oz)

2

Soft fruit (strawberries)

1 Choose firm red glossy fruit of equal size.

2 Wash, drain and hull.

3 Large strawberries are better sliced. Like smaller whole berries, they can be frozen in either 50% syrup or sugar pack. (See page 26)

4 Pack in rigid containers, leaving 1cm (½ inch) head-space. Top with crumpled foil if using syrup pack.

5 Strawberries can also be frozen crushed, with 100g (4oz) sugar added to each 450g (1 lb) fruit. Seal, label and freeze.

6 Possibly the best way to freeze strawberries, but a little more trouble, is to open freeze. Wash and hull berries, coat each carefully in sugar, space out on metal tray.

7 Place in freezer until frozen, then repack in polythene bags, withdrawing air.

8 Tie, label and freeze.

Storage limit	Thawing
12 months	*Refrigerator* 6–8 hours per 450g (1 lb) *Room temperature* 2–4 hours per 450g (1 lb)

1

2

Pictures 3 to 8, see over page

3

5

4

6

7

Stone fruit (cherries, plums, greengages etc.)

1 Wash and dry. Remove stalks and stones.
2 Freeze in sugar pack (see page 26) or 40–50% syrup according to the sweetness of the fruit. Pack in rigid containers.
3 Leave 1cm (½ inch) headspace. If using syrup pack, top with crumpled foil. Seal, label and freeze.

Storage limit	Thawing
12 months	*Refrigerator*
	6–8 hours per 225g
	(8oz)
	Room temperature
	2–4 hours per 225g
	(8oz)

8

1

Pictures 2 and 3, see over page

2

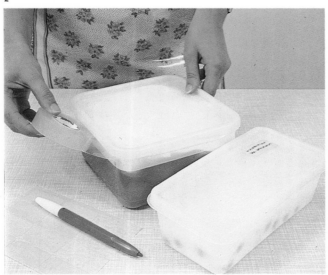

3

Stone fruit (peaches)

1 Wash and dry. Immerse in boiling water to facilitate skinning. Remove stone.

2 Slice into 40% syrup to which 2 teaspoons ascorbic acid per 600ml (1 pint) have been added, to prevent discoloration.

3 Alternatively, use sugar pack, first sprinkling the peach slices with ascorbic acid dissolved in water. Pack in rigid containers, leaving 1cm (½ inch) headspace. If using syrup pack, top with crumpled foil. Seal, label and freeze.

Storage limit	**Thawing**
12 months	*Refrigerator*
	6–8 hours per 225g
	(8oz)
	Room temperature
	2–4 hours per 225g (8oz)

1

Stone fruit (apricots)

1 Wash and dry. Immerse in boiling water to facilitate skinning. Remove stone.
2 Slice into 40% syrup to which 2 teaspoons ascorbic acid per 600ml (1 pint) have been added, to prevent discoloration.
3 Alternatively, use sugar pack, first sprinkling the apricot slices with ascorbic acid dissolved in water. Pack in rigid containers, leaving headspace. If using syrup pack, top with crumpled foil. Seal, label and freeze.

Storage limit	Thawing
12 months	*Refrigerator* 6–8 hours per 225g (8oz) *Room temperature* 2–4 hours per 225g (8oz)

2

3

VEGETABLES

Asparagus

1 Choose young stems with compact heads. Wash and trim, sort into sizes.

2 Blanch small spears for 2 minutes; medium spears for 3 minutes; large spears for 4 minutes.

3 Cool and drain. Pack 'head-to-tail' in rigid containers, leaving 2.5cm (1 inch) headspace. Seal, label and freeze.

Storage limit	**Thawing**
12 months	Unnecessary

2

1

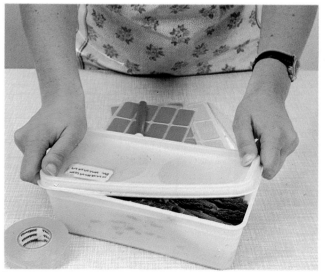

3

Aubergine

1 Choose sound fresh aubergines, rejecting any with brown spots. Peel, slice into equal-sized pieces.
2 Blanch for 4 minutes. Cool and drain.
3 Pack in rigid containers, leaving 2.5 cm (1 inch) head-space, or polythene bags, withdrawing air. Seal or tie, label and freeze.

Storage limit	Thawing
12 months	Unnecessary

2

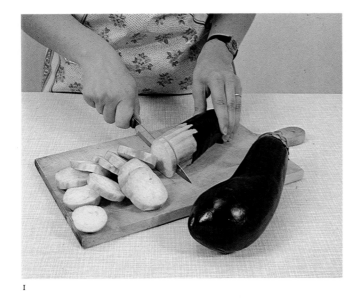

1

3

Beans, green (French or runner)

1 Choose fresh young beans that 'snap' when broken. Wash, string if necessary, cut or slice, or freeze whole if small enough.
2 Blanch sliced for 1 minute; cut for 2 minutes; whole for 3 minutes. Cool and drain.
3 Pack in polythene bags, withdrawing air. Tie, label and freeze.

Storage limit	Thawing
12 months	Unnecessary

2

1

3

Beans, broad

1 Choose small unblemished beans, pod and wash them.
2 Blanch for 3 minutes. Cool and drain.
3 Pack in rigid containers or polythene bags. Seal or tie, label and freeze.

Storage limit	**Thawing**
12 months	Unnecessary

2

1

3

Beetroot

1 Cook small beetroot, approx 7.5cm (3 inches) across, in boiling water 25–30 minutes, until tender. Drain and cool. Skin.
2 Pack in polythene bags, withdrawing air. Tie, label and freeze.

Storage limit	**Thawing**
6 months	*Refrigerator*
	6–8 hours
	Room temperature
	2–4 hours

2

1

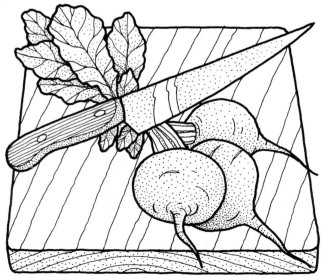

Brussels sprouts

1 Choose small compact sprouts, without yellowing. Trim, wash and grade for size.
2 Blanch small sprouts for 3 minutes; medium sprouts for 4 minutes. Cool and drain.
3 Pack in polythene bags, withdrawing air. Tie, label and freeze.

Storage limit	**Thawing**
12 months	Unnecessary

2

1

3

Cabbage

1 Freeze firm, solid cabbage only. Trim, separate leaves, shred or cut into wedges.
2 Blanch shredded for 1½ minutes; leaves for 2 minutes; wedges for 3 minutes; cool and drain.
3 Pack in polythene bags, withdrawing air. Tie, label and containers, leaving 1cm (½ inch) headspace. Tie or seal, label and freeze.

Storage limit	**Thawing**
6 months	Unnecessary. *Note* Once frozen, cabbage cannot be used for coleslaw or other salad.

2

1

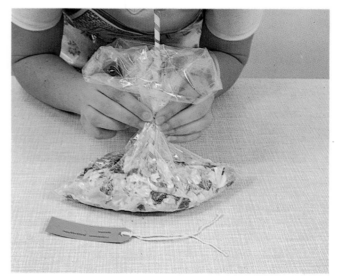

3

Carrots

1 Carrots are available all the year round, so it is only worth freezing them when very young. Trim, wash, scrape or scrub. Slice or freeze whole.

2 Blanch sliced for 3 minutes; whole for 4 minutes; cool and drain.

3 Pack in polythene bags, withdrawing air. Tie, label and freeze.

Storage limit	Thawing
12 months	Unnecessary

2

1

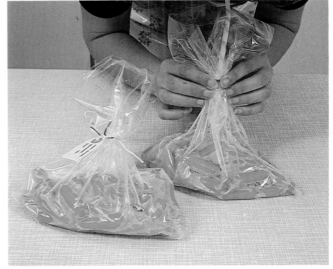

3

Cauliflower and broccoli

1 Choose firm heads. Trim, separate into florets, soak in salt solution, 1 tablespoon salt to 600ml (1 pint) water, for 30 minutes.
2 Blanch in salt solution as for soaking for 3 minutes. Cool and drain.
3 Pack in polythene bags, withdrawing air, or in rigid containers without leaving headspace. Tie or seal, label and freeze.

Storage limit		Thawing
Cauliflower	6 months	Unnecessary
Broccoli	12 months	

2

1

3

Celery

1 Choose firm crisp heads. Trim, cut into 2.5cm (1 inch) pieces.
2 Blanch for 3 minutes. Cool and drain.
3 Pack in polythene bags, withdrawing air, or in rigid containers, leaving 1cm (½ inch) headspace. Tie or seal, label and freeze.

Storage limit	**Thawing**
12 months	Unnecessary. Once frozen, celery cannot be eaten raw.

2

1

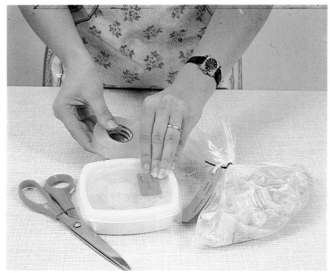

3

Mushrooms

1 Pick over carefully, discarding any which are mouldy or decayed. Skin, grade according to size; slice large ones. Dip in lemon juice to preserve colour.

2 Blanch whole for 30 seconds; buttons and slices for 20 seconds. Cool and drain.

3 Alternatively, mushrooms can be sautéed in butter or margarine, in which case no blanching is needed.

4 Pack in rigid containers, leaving 1cm (½ inch) head-space.

5 Seal, label and freeze.

Storage limit	**Thawing**
3 months	Unnecessary

2

3

4

Peas

1 Use very young perfect peas. Shell. Blanch for 1–1½ minutes according to size, using stockinette instead of wire basket.

2 Cool and drain.

3 Pack in polythene bags, withdrawing air, or in rigid containers, leaving 1cm (½ inch) headspace. Tie or seal, label and freeze.

Storage limit	Thawing
12 months	Unnecessary

5

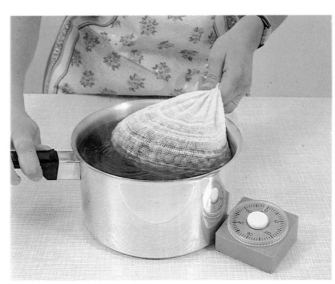

1

Pictures 2 and 3, see over page

2

3

Potatoes (chips)

1 Peel potatoes, and cut into chips. Blanch in hot deep fat until soft, but not coloured.
2 Pack in polythene bags, withdrawing air. Tie, label and freeze.

Storage limit	Thawing
6 months	*Refrigerator* 6–8 hours *Room temperature* 2–4 hours per 450g (1 lb) After thawing, deep fry until golden brown.

1

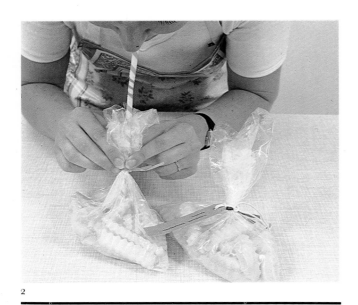

2

Potatoes (new)

1 Choose very small potatoes. Scrape them and boil until
cooked. Drain and cool.

2 Pack in polythene bags, withdrawing air. Tie, label and
freeze.

Storage limit
1 month

Thawing
Unnecessary

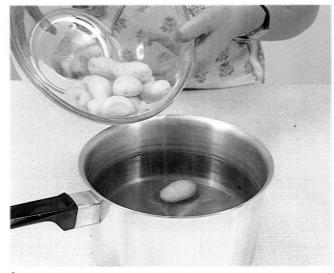

1

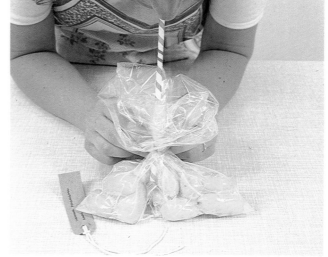

2

Peppers

1 Choose shiny, unwrinkled red or green peppers. Wash, trim, core, deseed, halve or slice.
2 Blanch, if to be cooked after thawing, for 2–3 minutes. Cool and drain. If to be used raw after thawing, do not blanch.
3 Pack in polythene bags, withdrawing air, or in rigid containers, leaving a 1cm (½ inch) headspace. Tie or seal, label and freeze.

Storage limit	*Refrigerator*
12 months	6–8 hours per 450g
Thawing	(1 lb)
Unnecessary if to be	*Room temperature*
cooked. Otherwise:	2–4 hours per 450g
	(1lb)

2

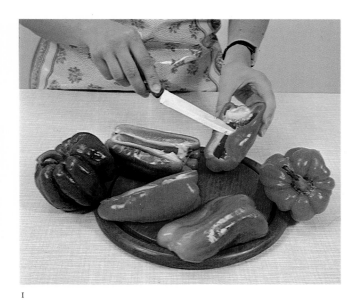

1

3

Root vegetables (parsnips, turnips, swedes)

1 Choose young fresh roots. Wash, peel and dice into even-sized pieces.
2 Blanch for 2–2½ minutes, according to size of pieces. Cool and drain.
3 Pack in polythene bags, withdrawing air. Tie, label and freeze.

Storage limit	**Thawing**
12 months	Unnecessary

2

1

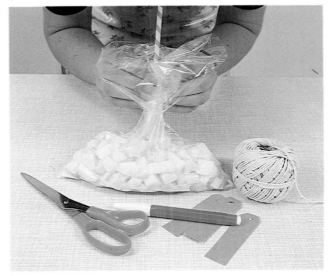

3

Spinach

1 Choose fresh, tender spinach. Wash well; trim off stalks.
2 Blanch for 2 minutes, shaking to separate leaves. Cool and drain.
3 Pack in rigid containers, leaving 2.5cm (1 inch) head-space. Seal, label and freeze.

Storage limit	**Thawing**
12 months	Unnecessary

2

1

3

Tomato purée

1 Choose ripe but firm tomatoes without soft spots. Skin and quarter. Cook slowly without adding water.
2 Press through a fine sieve when cooked.
3 Pack in rigid containers, leaving 2.5cm (1 inch) head-space.
4 Seal, label and freeze.

Storage limit	**Thawing**
12 months	Unnecessary if used for cooking

Tomato pulp

Tomato pulp can be frozen as above, but sieving is unnecessary.

2

1

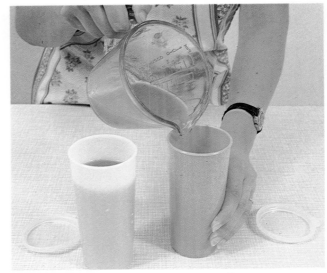

3

Picture 4, see over page

PASTRY

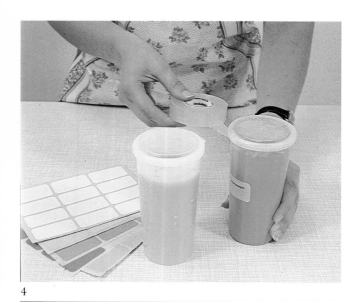

4

1

2

Pastry, uncooked dough

1 Mix to usual recipe, flour well, but do not roll out. Cut to suitable size.
2 Pack in polythene bag, withdrawing air.
3 Tie, label, stating type of pastry (shortcrust, puff, etc.), and freeze.

Storage limit	Thawing
3 months	*Refrigerator*
	8–10 hours

3

Pastry, uncooked, prepared

1 Mix to usual recipe, roll out, cut to required shape and size for pies, tarts, etc.
2 Stand shaped pastry on suitably sized cardboard, place foil or freezer paper in between each pastry layer. Overwrap, seal, label and freeze.

Storage limit	Thawing
3 months	Until workable

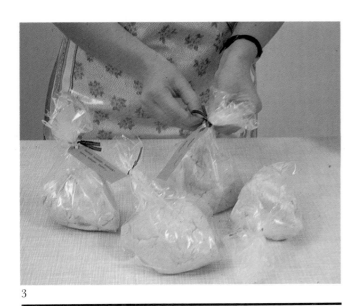

1

2

BREAD

Bread, commercially baked, wrapped (this page)

1 Wrapped bread keeps better in the freezer if overwrapped with clingfilm or freezer paper.
2 Seal, label and freeze.

Storage limit	Thawing
6 months	Remove overwrap, leave in commercial wrap 4–5 hours

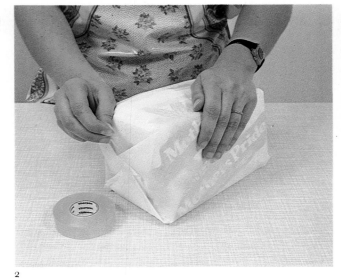

2

Bread, commercially baked, unwrapped (page 91)

1 Even if well wrapped in clingfilm, such breads as French and Vienna lose their crispness after 3 days.
2 Overwrap in freezer paper. Seal, label and freeze.

Storage limit	Thawing
4–6 weeks	In wrapper 3–4 hours

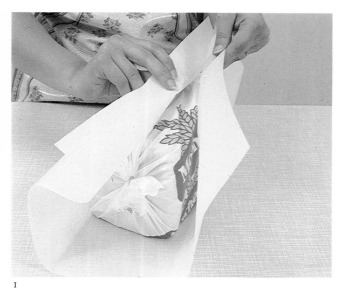

1

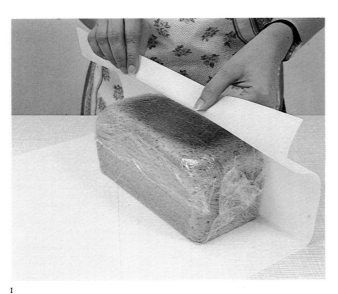

1

Bread, home-baked (below)
1 Bake bread to your usual recipe. *Cool thoroughly* before wrapping in clingfilm. Seal, label and freeze.

Storage limit	Thawing
6 weeks	In wrapper 3–4 hours

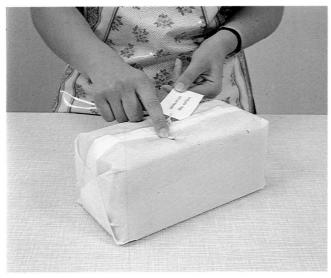

2

1

Bread dough, unrisen

1 Follow recipe instructions, kneading well, but do not set to rise.
2 Grease the inside of polythene bags, to prevent dough sticking. Divide dough into convenient 'one-loaf' sizes, one to a bag.
3 Withdraw as much air as possible from the bag, leaving only enough space for the dough to rise slightly before it freezes.
4 Seal, label and freeze.

Storage limit	Thawing
8 weeks	In bag, 8–10 hours. *Note* Risen dough can be frozen, but its extra bulk wastes freezer space.

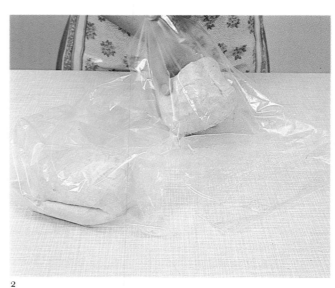

2

1

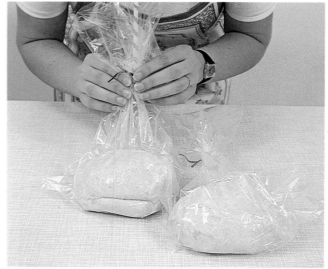

3

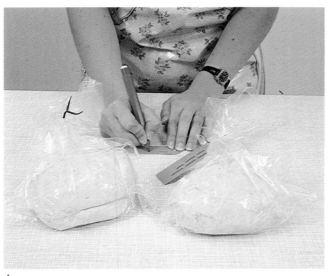

4

Sandwiches

1 Prepare sandwiches, but don't use lettuce or celery, which wilt, or hard-boiled eggs, which go tough.

2 Make up conveniently sized packs and wrap in cling-film.

3 Overwrap with freezer paper. Remember to state the type of filling on the label. Nothing is more infuriating than an anonymous sandwich.

Storage limit	Thawing
4 weeks	In wrapper 2½–3 hours, according to thickness

1

2

Picture 3, see over page

CAKES

3

Sponges, iced or plain

1 Make sponge to usual recipe, *cool thoroughly*. If iced, make sure icing is completely set before wrapping in clingfilm.

2 See page 35 for instructions for making a round parcel. Seal, label and freeze.

Storage limit	Thawing
Fatless sponge 10 months	*Room temperature*
Others 4 months	In wrapper 3–4 hours
	Note American boiled frosting does not freeze well

1

2

Cakes, iced or plain

1 & 2 Package and freeze as for sponges.

Storage limit	**Thawing**
4 months	*Room temperature* In wrapper 3–4 hours

1

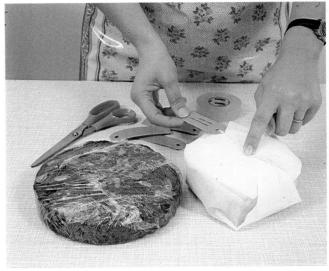

2

EGGS AND DAIRY PRODUCE

Eggs, whole egg mixture

1 Beat eggs lightly without making them frothy. Add *either* 3 tablespoons sugar *or* ½ teaspoon salt to 900ml (1½ pints) egg mixture.

2 Freeze in convenient amounts in rigid containers, leaving 1–2.5cm (½–1 inch) headspace in wide containers, 2.5cm (1 inch) headspace in narrow containers.

3 Seal. When labelling, remember to state whether sugar or salt has been added. Freeze.

4 Egg yolks can be frozen as whole egg mixture. Egg whites can be frozen without the addition of sugar or salt.

Storage limit   *Room temperature*
6 months   3 hours per 600ml (1 pint)
Thawing
Refrigerator
18–20 hours per 600ml (1 pint)

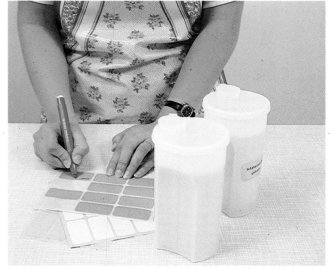

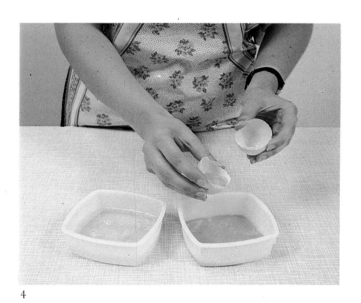

4

Milk, very fresh homogenized or skimmed only

1 Use suitable cartons, leaving 5cm (2 inch) headspace per 600ml (1 pint).
2 Empty milk or fruit juice cartons can be used if thoroughly cleaned. It is advisable to staple them before sealing. Label and freeze.

Storage limit	Thawing
1 month	*Refrigerator*
	20 hours per 600ml
	(1 pint)
	Room temperature
	2 hours per 600ml
	(1 pint)

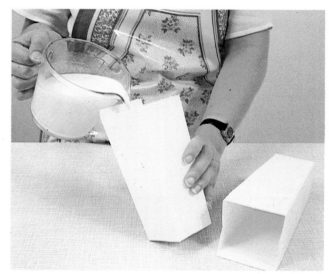

1

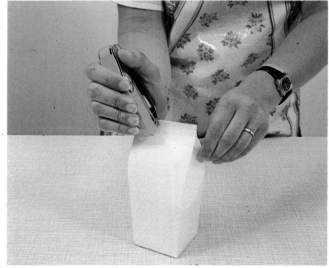

2

Cream, double or pasteurized clotted

1 Use very fresh cream only, and freeze as quickly as possible. If bought in containers, overwrap if you feel it necessary. Seal or tie, label and freeze.

Storage limit	Thawing
4 months	*Refrigerator*
	12 hours per 150ml
	(¼ pint)
	Room temperature
	2 hours per 150ml
	(¼ pint)

Butter, commercial

1 Only freeze butter that hasn't softened at any time. Leave in original wrappings, and overwrap. Seal, label and freeze.

Storage limit	Thawing
Salted 6 months	*Refrigerator*
Unsalted 12 months	2 hours per 450g (1 lb)
	Room temperature
	1 hour per 450g (1 lb)
	Note Home-made butter
	can be frozen if made
	from pasteurized cream.

1

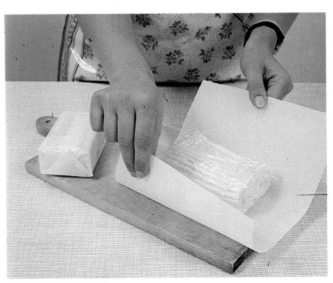

1

Cheese, hard

1 Divide cheese into conveniently sized portions, not exceeding 225g (8oz).
2 Wrap cheese very carefully, or it will dry out, or contaminate other foods.
3 Use clingfilm first, and then overwrap with foil or freezer paper.
4 Seal, label and freeze.

Storage limit	**Thawing**
4–6 months	*Refrigerator*
	8 hours per 225g (8oz)
	Room temperature
	2–3 hours per 225g (8oz)
	Note Thawed cheese is usually crumbly, and only suitable for cooking

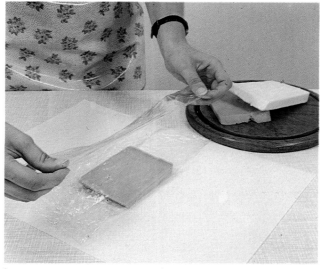

2

1

3

Picture 4, see over page

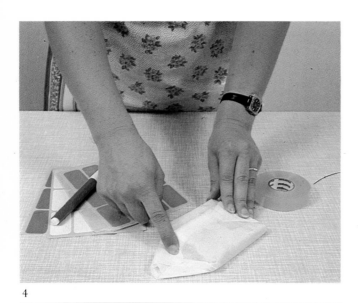

4

Cheese dips

1 Prepare to usual recipe, pack in rigid containers, leaving 2.5cm (1 inch) headspace. Seal, label and freeze.

Storage limit	Thawing
2 months	*Refrigerator*
	8 hours per 100g (4oz)
	Room temperature
	2–3 hours per 100g
	(4oz)

1

Casserole & stews

1 Line a casserole dish with foil, overlapping sides by about 5cm (2 inches). Place cooked food inside.
2 Cover with a sheet of foil; seal by pinching edges together. Seal, label and freeze.
3 After freezing, lift out foil-wrapped parcel.
4 Cut food block into meal-sized portions.
5 Wrap each portion separately. Seal, label and freeze.

Storage limit
2 months

Thawing
Cook from frozen:
1 hour at 400°F/200°C/Mark 6
or until hot right through

2

1

3

Pictures 4 and 5, see over page

4

Pies

1 Don't cut vents in the crusts of pies to be frozen. Cool thoroughly before freezing. Pies can be placed in polythene bags, or wrapped first in clingfilm.

2 Overwrap in foil. If using bag method, remember to withdraw air with a straw.

3 Seal or tie, label and freeze.

Storage limit	**Thawing**
2 months	Cook from frozen: about 1 hour at 425°F/220°C/Mark 7 according to size

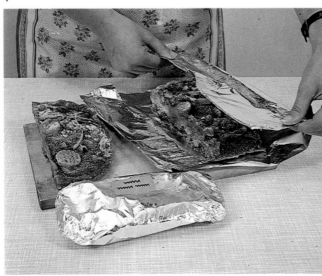

5

1

1

3

2

Puddings

1 Wrap boiled or steamed puddings in clingfilm. Over-wrap with foil.
2 Seal, label and freeze.

2

1

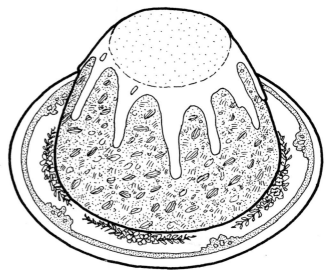

Recipes

There are hundreds – perhaps thousands – of meals that can be created and then frozen. The recipes that follow have been chosen firstly because they freeze well, secondly because they use a wide range of interesting ingredients, and thirdly because I like them, and I hope sincerely that you will, too. From this selection it should be possible for you to choose meals for all occasions – from catering for the sudden arrival of your children's hungry friends, to that special dinner party where you can delight your guests with exciting dishes, all from your freezer. You need not stop here, of course, providing you follow the few rules laid down in this book you will find that you can prepare, cook and freeze almost all of your favourite meals.

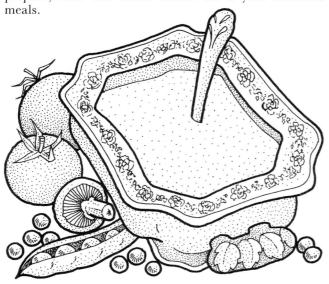

SOUPS

Pea soup (Serves 4–6)

	METRIC	IMPERIAL	AMERICAN
Peas, frozen or fresh	*450g*	*1 lb*	*1 lb*
Chicken or ham stock	*600ml*	*1 pt*	*2½ cups*
Fresh mint, chopped	*2 tsp*	*2 tsp*	*2 tsp*
Sugar	*1 tsp*	*1 tsp*	*1 tsp*
Butter or margarine	*25g*	*1 oz*	*2 tbsp*
Flour, plain	*25g*	*1 oz*	*¼ cup*
Milk	*300ml*	*½ pt*	*1¼ cups*
Salt and pepper			

While bringing the peas to the boil in the stock, chop the mint with the sugar. Put half the mint and sugar in with the peas. Cover the pan and simmer for 20 minutes or until the peas are very tender. Do not drain.

Make a sauce with the butter, flour and milk. Bring to the boil, stirring, then season to taste. Simmer for 5 minutes, stirring.

Liquidize or purée the peas in their stock, then stir into the sauce, adding a little more liquid if required. Reheat if necessary, serve sprinkled with the remaining chopped fresh mint; float a little cream or yoghurt on top, if liked.

Cooking time 30 minutes

To freeze   Cool, pack in rigid containers or polythene bags. Seal or tie, label and freeze. *Storage limit* 1 month.

Thawing   Unnecessary, if heated slowly, stirring. Season and garnish.

Tomato soup (Serves 4–6)

	METRIC	IMPERIAL	AMERICAN
Ripe tomatoes, quartered	*1kg*	*2 lb*	*2 lb*
Onion, chopped	*1*	*1*	*1*
Sage, preferably fresh, chopped	*1 tsp*	*1 tsp*	*1 tsp*
Parsley sprigs	*6*	*6*	*6*
Chicken stock	*900ml*	*1½ pt*	*3¾ cups*
Salt and pepper			

Add the tomatoes, onion, sage and parsley to the stock. Season, bring to the boil, and simmer uncovered for 40 minutes. Blend or rub through a fine sieve.

Cooking time 50 minutes
To freeze   Cool, pack in rigid containers or polythene bags. Seal or tie, label and freeze. *Storage limit* 1 month.
Thawing   Unnecessary, if heated slowly, stirring.

Borsch (Serves 6–8)

	METRIC	IMPERIAL	AMERICAN
Butter	*50g*	*2 oz*	*¼ cup*
Medium onion, chopped	*1*	*1*	*1*
Beetroot, uncooked and grated	*225g*	*8oz*	*½ lb*
Tomatoes, chopped	*2*	*2*	*2*
Potato, grated	*1*	*1*	*1*
Clove garlic, crushed (optional)	*1*	*1*	*1*
Beef stock	*1.2 litres*	*2 pt*	*5 cups*
Cabbage, shredded	*225g*	*8 oz*	*½ lb*
Vinegar	*2 tbsp*	*2tbsp*	*2tbsp*
Salt and pepper			
Fresh dill leaves or parsley, chopped	*½ tbsp*	*½ tbsp*	*½ tbsp*

Melt the butter and gently fry the onion for 5 minutes. Add the beetroot, tomato, potato and garlic, cook for 15 minutes in half the stock.

Add the rest of the stock, cabbage, vinegar and seasoning, and simmer for 30 minutes. Serve sprinkled with dill or parsley.

Note If this recipe seems more elaborate than others, it should be pointed out that this is a good hearty Borsch, practically a meal in itself.

Cooking time 1 hour
To freeze   Cool, do not add dill or parsley. Pack in rigid containers or polythene bags. Seal or tie, label and freeze. *Storage limit* 1 month.
Thawing   Unnecessary, if heated slowly, stirring.

Curry and rice soup (Serves 4–6)

	METRIC	IMPERIAL	AMERICAN
Butter or margarine	*25g*	*1 oz*	*2 tbsp*
Onion, chopped	*1*	*1*	*1*
Curry powder	*1 tbsp*	*1 tbsp*	*1 tbsp*
Flour, plain	*1 tbsp*	*1 tbsp*	*1 tbsp*
Chicken stock	*900ml*	*1½ pt*	*3¾ cups*
Sticks celery, sliced	*2*	*2*	*2*
Rice, long-grain	*50g*	*2 oz*	*⅓ cup*

Melt the butter or margarine and gently fry the onion until soft. Add the curry powder and cook for 2 minutes. Stir in the flour and add the stock. Bring to the boil, stirring, and add the celery and rice. Simmer for about 15 minutes, until the rice is tender.

Cooking time 25 minutes
To freeze   Cool, pack in rigid containers or polythene bags. Seal or tie, label and freeze. *Storage limit* 1 month.
Thawing   Unnecessary, if heated slowly, stirring.

STARTERS

Orange scallops (Serves 6)

	METRIC	IMPERIAL	AMERICAN
Orange	*1*	*1*	*1*
Scallops	*6*	*6*	*6*
Fish stock	*300ml*	*½ pt*	*1¼ cups*
Salt and pepper			
Butter	*15g*	*½ oz*	*1 tbsp*

Peel the orange very thinly, and cut the peel into julienne strips. Squeeze the orange. Cover the scallops with fish stock, adding seasoning and julienne strips. Cook gently until the scallop white becomes solid.

Remove the scallops and add the butter and orange juice to the stock. Serve with lightly braised mixed vegetables, covered with the orange sauce.

Note This dish can be made with frozen scallops.

Cooking time 20 minutes

To freeze   Cool, pack in rigid containers. Seal, label and freeze. *Storage limit* 1 month.

Thawing   In refrigerator for 4 hours. Heat through before serving.

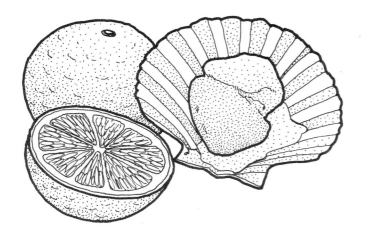

Ratatouille tart (Serves 6)

	METRIC	IMPERIAL	AMERICAN
Aubergine, peeled and sliced	*1*	*1*	*1*
Courgettes, peeled and sliced	*225g*	*8 oz*	*½ lb*
Cooking oil	*3 tbsp*	*3 tbsp*	*3 tbsp*
Onion, sliced	*½*	*½*	*½*
Clove garlic, crushed (optional)	*1*	*1*	*1*
Bouquet garni	*1*	*1*	*1*
Tomatoes, skinned, deseeded and sliced	*225g*	*8 oz*	*½ lb*
Salt and pepper			
Green or red pepper, thinly sliced	*1*	*1*	*1*
Pastry to make 12 tartlet cases (using about 100g (4 oz) etc.)			

Sprinkle the aubergines and courgettes with salt and leave, covered by a plate, for 1 hour.

Heat the oil in a heavy pan and fry the onion until slightly coloured. Add the garlic and cook for 5 minutes, then add the remaining filling ingredients. Cook slowly, covered, for about 30 minutes. Remove the bouquet garni.

Meanwhile, bake the tartlet cases blind in a preheated moderately hot oven (200°C, 400°F, Gas mark 6). When the ratatouille is ready, fill the tartlets and serve warm.

Cooking time 1 hour

To freeze   Both ratatouille and pastry freeze well, and it is possible to either freeze them separately or freeze the filled tartlets, to be warmed through when required. *Storage limit* 3 months if garlic omitted, otherwise 1 month.

Thawing   At room temperature for 3 hours.

Potted lobster (Serves 4)

	METRIC	IMPERIAL	AMERICAN
Butter	100g	4 oz	1/2 cup
Black pepper, freshly ground	1 tsp	1 tsp	1 tsp
Pinch cayenne pepper			
Ground mace	1 tsp	1 tsp	1 tsp
Lobster meat, cooked	225g	8 oz	1/2 cup
Juice of 1/2 lemon			

Melt 1 tablespoon of the butter and add the peppers and mace, then the lobster and lemon juice. Heat through, stirring, but do not brown.

Pack in waxed containers or cartons, leaving a headspace. Melt remaining butter and pour over the packed lobster, making sure it is covered completely. Serve on toast, garnished with parsley and lemon slices.

Note Crabmeat, prawns or shrimps can be used instead of lobster.

To freeze *Seal, label and freeze. Storage limit 1 month.*
Thawing Overnight in refrigerator.

FISH

Cod en papillote (Serves 4)

	METRIC	IMPERIAL	AMERICAN
Cod steaks	4	4	4
Butter	65g	2 1/2 oz	5 tbsp
Onion, chopped	1	1	1
Button mushrooms, sliced	225g	8 oz	2 cups
Tomatoes, large, skinned and sliced	2	2	2
Salt and pepper			
Natural yoghurt	4 tbsp	4 tbsp	4 tbsp
Pinch dried thyme			

Take four double-thickness pieces of foil, each large enough to parcel up a single piece of cod. Butter the foil generously on one side, and lay the cod on the buttered side.

Fry the onion in the remaining butter for 2–3 minutes, add the mushrooms and fry for a further minute. Cover the fish with this mixture. Add the tomatoes, seasoning, yoghurt and thyme to each. Bring the edges of the foil together, and fold over along the edges to make a fairly loose moistureproof parcel. Place on a baking tray and bake in a preheated moderately hot oven (200°C, 400°F, Gas Mark 6) for about 35 minutes. Unwrap and serve.

Cooking time 45 minutes
To freeze   Since the fish is already wrapped in foil, simply cool well, overwrap, label and freeze. *Storage limit* 2 months.
Thawing   Unnecessary if you are careful to heat your foil parcels right through.

Orange plaice (Serves 4)

	METRIC	IMPERIAL	AMERICAN
Oranges	2	2	2
Mayonnaise	150ml	1/4 pt	2/3 cup
Plaice fillets, small	8	8	8
Watercress to garnish			

Grate the rind of the oranges, squeezing the juice from one half of an orange, reserving the rest for slicing. Mix the juice and grated rind with the mayonnaise.

Remove the dark skin from the fish, and roll the fillets up, placing them on a buttered pie plate. Cover and steam over a saucepan of boiling water until tender – 10 to 20 minutes according to size.

Arrange the cooled fillets on a serving dish, coat with the mayonnaise and place orange slices around the edge of the dish. Garnish with watercress, and serve with salad. Can be used as a summer main course or as a starter.

Cooking time	15–20 minutes
To freeze	This dish can be made from frozen fillets, completely defrosted before poaching. The cooked fillets can also be frozen without the addition of the mayonnaise. *Storage limit* 3 months.
Thawing	In the refrigerator for 6 hours per 450g (1 lb). Cover with mayonnaise and garnish.

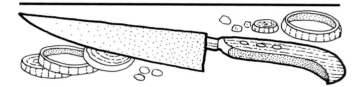

Salmon

	METRIC	IMPERIAL	AMERICAN
Salmon	1	1	1
Vinegar	1 tbsp	1 tbsp	1 tbsp
Olive oil	1 tbsp	1 tbsp	1 tbsp
Bay leaves	2	2	2
Peppercorns (see method)	4	4	4
Fennel	½ tsp	½ tsp	½ tsp
Pinch salt			

If you don't have a fish kettle with a lifting tray inside, line a large pan with butter muslin with which to lift the cooked fish without breaking it. The pan *must* be large enough for the fish to lie absolutely straight. Add all ingredients, making sure that the fish is completely covered with water (Add 4 peppercorns to each litre (2 pints) of water used.)

Bring to the boil *slowly* and then gently simmer for about 5 minutes. Test by prodding with the end of a thin bladed knife somewhere where it won't show. Remove from the heat and leave to cool in the cooking liquid.

Note If you are using a frozen fish, it must be completely defrosted before you start to cook it. Sea trout can be cooked in the same way.

Cooking time	About 1 hour, according to size
To freeze	Cooked fish breaks very easily, and its appearance can be spoilt by too much handling. If you really need to freeze it, lay it on foil in the pan, so that it can be lifted out, drained, cooled, and frozen with as little handling as possible. Overwrap when frozen. *Storage limit* 2 months.
Thawing	In the refrigerator, 6–10 hours per 450g (1 lb) according to size. If serving cold, make sure that the fish is completely thawed right through.

Mackerel with mint (Serves 4)

	METRIC	IMPERIAL	AMERICAN
Mackerel	4	4	4
Sprigs mint			
Cooking oil	1 tbsp	1 tbsp	1 tbsp
Mayonnaise	300ml	½ pt	1¼ cups
Mint sauce, concentrated	1 tbsp	1 tbsp	1 tbsp

Clean and gut the fish, and cut off the fins with scissors. Wash and dry the inside. Make 3 slashes with a sharp knife on each side of the fish. Place sprigs of fresh mint in each gash, bruising the leaves first. Brush the fish with the oil and grill for about 5 minutes on each side.

Serve either cold or hot, with a generous spoonful of mayonnaise to which you have added the mint sauce concentrate.

Cooking time	20 minutes
To freeze	Omit the mayonnaise; cool the fish, wrap flat, overwrap. Seal, label and freeze. *Storage limit* 1 month.
Thawing	In refrigerator for 6 hours per 450g (1 lb), then heat through thoroughly unless being eaten cold. Dress with mayonnaise.

MEAT

Moussaka (Serves 6)

	METRIC	IMPERIAL	AMERICAN
Potatoes, sliced	1 kg	2 lb	2 lb
Aubergines, peeled and sliced	450g	1 lb	1 lb
Tomatoes, fresh or canned	450g	1 lb	1 lb
Oil	2 tbsp	2 tbsp	2 tbsp
Onions, chopped	3	3	3
Clove garlic, crushed (optional)	1	1	1
Minced lamb or beef	750g	1½ lb	1½ lb
Courgettes, sliced	450g	1 lb	1 lb
Salt and pepper			

Cheese sauce

	METRIC	IMPERIAL	AMERICAN
Butter or margarine	50g	2 oz	¼ cup
Flour, plain	50g	2 oz	½ cup
Milk	600ml	1 pt	2½ cups
Cheddar cheese, grated	350g	12 oz	3 cups

Boil the potatoes until just tender. Boil the aubergines for a couple of minutes only. If using fresh tomatoes, skin and seed them. Heat the oil in a heavy pan and soften the onions, garlic and tomatoes. Add the mince and brown. Season, cover the pan and cook for about 25 minutes; check occasionally that the mixture isn't burning.

In a casserole, layer the aubergines, courgettes and potato, add a layer of meat, and then another layer of aubergines, courgettes and potato. Prepare the cheese sauce and pour over the top. Place in a preheated cool oven (150°C, 300°F, Gas Mark 2) for 2 hours at least – it improves with long slow cooking. If the top doesn't brown nicely, pop it under a hot grill for a minute or two.

Note This is a good dish to make from your frozen vegetables and bulk-cooked mince.

Cooking time 3 hours

To freeze Cook in a foil-lined casserole (see page 101) if you plan to freeze this dish. *Storage limit* 1 month if garlic is included, otherwise 2 months.

Thawing Unnecessary, but heat through slowly but thoroughly.

Liver with mint and red wine (Serves 4)

	METRIC	IMPERIAL	AMERICAN
Butter	25g	1 oz	2 tbsp
Onions, thinly sliced	2	2	2
Calves' liver	450g	1 lb	1 lb
Salt and freshly ground black pepper			
Fresh mint, chopped	1 tsp	1 tsp	1 tsp
Wine glass red wine	½	½	½

Melt the butter and fry the onions until soft. Add the liver to the pan, sprinkling with salt, pepper and chopped mint first on one side and then on the other as you turn the slices over. Fry for about 3–4 minutes on each side until cooked, then add the wine, shaking the pan to distribute it. Cook for a couple of minutes more; serve immediately.

Cooking time 15 minutes

To freeze Cool, pack in rigid containers. Seal, label and freeze. *Storage limit* 2 months.

Thawing In refrigerator for 4 hours per 450g (1 lb).

Colonial goose (Serves 6)

	METRIC	IMPERIAL	AMERICAN
Shoulder of lamb,			
boned	*1*	*1*	*1*
Stuffing			
Butter or margarine	*50g*	*2oz*	*¼ cup*
Honey, clear	*1 tbsp*	*1 tbsp*	*1 tbsp*
Dried apricots,			
chopped	*1 tbsp*	*1 tbsp*	*1 tbsp*
Fresh breadcrumbs	*100g*	*4 oz*	*2 cups*
Onion, minced or			
grated	*1*	*1*	*1*
Dried mixed herbs	*1 tsp*	*1 tsp*	*1 tsp*
Salt and pepper			
Egg, beaten	*1*	*1*	*1*
Marinade			
Wine glass red wine	*1*	*1*	*1*
Wine glass wine			
vinegar	*1*	*1*	*1*
Honey, clear	*1 tbsp*	*1 tbsp*	*1 tbsp*
Bay leaf	*1*	*1*	*1*
Peppercorns	*6*	*6*	*6*
Clove garlic,			
crushed (optional)	*1*	*1*	*1*

Melt the butter and honey and add to the chopped apricots and breadcrumbs. Mix in the grated onion, herbs and seasoning. Bind with the beaten egg.

Trim any excess fat from the joint, spoon the stuffing into the cavity. Make sure the stuffing is packed well inside. Sew the edges of cavity together, using fine twine.

Mix the marinade ingredients together and marinate the joint in this for about 6 hours, turning and basting occasionally.

Remove from the marinade. Roast in a preheated moderate oven (180°C, 350°F, Gas Mark 4) for approximately 20 minutes per 450g (1 lb) meat, covering with foil if the skin begins to brown too quickly. The marinade can be added to the gravy if liked, but taste while cooking, as it is very vinegary.

Cooking time 8 hours (including marinating)
To freeze Cool, wrap in clingfilm and then over-wrap. Seal, label and freeze. *Storage limit 1 month.*
Thawing Overnight in the refrigerator.

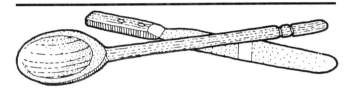

Pork chops with port (Serves 4)

	METRIC	IMPERIAL	AMERICAN
Olive oil	*1 tbsp*	*1 tbsp*	*1 tbsp*
Pork chops	*4*	*4*	*4*
Onions, chopped	*2*	*2*	*2*
Tomatoes, skinned			
and chopped	*225g*	*8 oz*	*½ lb*
Fresh rosemary	*2 tsp*	*2 tsp*	*2 tsp*
Salt and pepper			
Wine glass port or			
sweet red wine	*1*	*1*	*1*

Heat the oil in a heavy frying pan and brown the chops on both sides. Transfer the chops to a casserole. Fry the onions until transparent. Stir in the tomatoes, rosemary and seasoning. Add the wine, stir until bubbling and pour over the chops. Bake in a preheated moderate oven (180°C, 350°F. Gas Mark 4) for about 20 minutes until the chops are tender.

Cooking time 35 minutes
To freeze Cool, skim off fat, pack in rigid container. Seal, label and freeze. *Storage limit 3 months.*
Thawing Bake in moderate oven, covered for about 30 minutes; uncover, bake for a further 5 minutes.

POULTRY

Honey duck (Serves 4–6)

	METRIC	IMPERIAL	AMERICAN
Duck, drawn and trussed	I	I	I
Stuffing			
Pork sausage meat	450g	1 lb	1 lb
Fresh breadcrumbs	50g	2oz	1 cup
Grated rind of 1 orange			
Dried mixed herbs	½ tsp	½ tsp	½ tsp
Salt and pepper			
Glaze			
Clear honey	1 tbsp	1 tbsp	1 tbsp
Juice of 1 orange			
Gravy			
Giblet stock (see method)	300 ml	½ pt	1¼ cups
Flour, plain	25g	1 oz	¼ cup
Salt and pepper			
Garnish			
Orange slices			
Watercress			

Mix the stuffing ingredients together. Pack into the duck, skewering or sewing down the loose skin, so that the stuffing doesn't escape during cooking.

Place the duck in a roasting tin, and prick the skin all over with a darning needle to allow the fat to escape. Rub the skin with salt. Roast in a preheated moderately hot oven (20°C, 400°F, Gas Mark 6) for 30 minutes, then reduce the temperature to 180°C, 350°F, Gas Mark 4, and cook for a further 1½ hours until nearly cooked.

Glaze with a mixture of the honey and orange juice, and return to the oven for not more than 15 minutes.

Prepare the stock by simmering the giblets in water for at least 1 hour; strain. When the duck is cooked, take the drippings from the pan and stir in the flour to make a paste. Add the stock, season well and cook until thickened, stirring all the time. Garnish with orange slices and watercress.

Cooking time 2½ hours

To freeze Best frozen unglazed, as much of the glaze will stick to wrapping paper. *Storage limit* 1 month.

Thawing At least 12 hours in refrigerator, until the centre is completely defrosted. Glaze, heat through thoroughly, garnish and serve.

Turkey supreme (Serves 3–4)

	METRIC	IMPERIAL	AMERICAN
Onion, small, sliced	I	I	I
Clove garlic, crushed	I	I	I
Pinch curry powder			
Tomato purée	1 tbsp	1 tbsp	1 tbsp
Lemon juice	½ tsp	½ tsp	½ tsp
Apricot jam	1 tbsp	1 tbsp	1 tbsp
Turkey, cooked and diced	225g	8 oz	½ lb
Salt and pepper			
Mayonnaise	300ml	½ pt	1¼ cups
Paprika			
Parsley sprigs			

Place the onion and garlic in a blender and blend for 1 minute. Place the curry powder, tomato purée, lemon juice and jam in a saucepan and bring slowly to the boil, stirring all the time. Add the onions and garlic and blend until smooth.

Add the diced turkey to the purée, season and fold in mayonnaise. Chill overnight, garnish with paprika and parsley just before serving with a green or rice salad.

Cooking time 20 minutes

To freeze Do not add mayonnaise; place mixture in rigid container. Seal, label and freeze. *Storage limit* 2 months.

Thawing In refrigerator for 4–5 hours, fold in mayonnaise, chill again.

Game hens (Serves 4)

	METRIC	IMPERIAL	AMERICAN
Game hens	2	2	2
Butter, melted	2 tbsp	2 tbsp	2 tbsp
Natural yoghurt	2 tbsp	2 tbsp	2 tbsp
Rosemary	½ tsp	½ tsp	½ tsp
Thyme	½ tsp	½ tsp	½ tsp
Black pepper corns, cracked	½ tsp	½ tsp	½ tsp
Salt			

Halve the birds down the back, then place in an ovenproof dish, flesh side up. Mix all the remaining ingredients together and brush the birds with the mixture. Bake, uncovered, in a preheated moderate oven (180°C, 350°F, Gas Mark 4) for 30 minutes, brushing over at least twice. Cover the dish and bake until the birds are tender, about another 30 minutes but depending on the size of the birds.
Note This recipe is also suitable for small chickens and smaller type of game birds.

Cooking time About 1 hour
To freeze Cool, pack in polythene boxes. Seal, label and freeze. *Storage limit* 2 months.
Thawing In refrigerator for 5–6 hours according to size. Heat through thoroughly in oven.

Poulet Normande (Serves 4–6)

	METRIC	IMPERIAL	AMERICAN
Butter	25g	1 oz	2 tbsp
Chicken joints	6	6	6
Onions, small, sliced	4	4	4
Mushrooms, sliced	175g	6 oz	1½ cups
Flour	25g	1 oz	¼ cup
Stewed apple purée	175g	6 oz	¾ cups
Chicken stock, seasoned	300ml	½ pt	1¼ cups
Wine glass white wine	½	½	½
Single cream	150ml	¼ pt	⅔ cup

Melt the butter in a heavy frying pan and brown the chicken joints. Transfer to a casserole. Fry the onions until light brown, then add the mushrooms. Sprinkle with the flour and gradually add the apple purée, then the stock and wine. When thickened, pour over the chicken joints. Bake in a preheated cool oven (150°C, 300°F, Gas Mark 2) for about 2 hours. Just before serving, stir in the cream.

Cooking time 2½ hours
To freeze Do not add cream. If cooking for the freezer, it is best to line the casserole dish with foil, as shown on page 101; so that the frozen chicken can be lifted out, over-wrapped, labelled and sealed, and the casserole dish put back into use. *Storage limit* 3 months.
Thawing No thawing required; simply heat right through gently, stirring in cream just before serving.

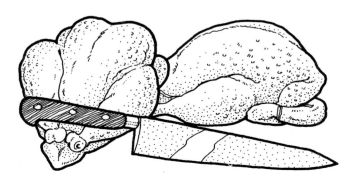

DESSERTS

Frozen cream (Serves 4)

	METRIC	IMPERIAL	AMERICAN
Eggs	3	3	3
Caster sugar	225g	8 oz	1 cup
Double cream	600ml	1 pt	2½ cups
Fresh raspberries	450g	1 lb	1 lb
Fresh peaches, sliced	2	2	2

Whisk the eggs lightly with the sugar. Stir in the cream, and freeze. You can, if you like, add flavouring before freezing, but the dessert has such a delightful creamy taste that I don't think it's really necessary.

Before serving, top with fresh whole raspberries or a purée of fresh raspberries, and fresh peach slices.

Note This is a marvellous dinner party dessert, and its rather high cost is off-set by the ease with which it is made. It can be frozen in the actual dishes in which it is to be served, if they will stand freezing, for instance silver or stainless steel coupes.

To freeze As above, in its own dishes. *Storage limit* I don't think it has ever been tested, because every time the freezer is opened, a little dish seems to disappear! It is meant to be made before a special occasion, but would probably store for 4 months, if given the chance.

Thawing Put in the refrigerator a couple of hours before serving – it should have the consistency of hard ice cream.

Coffee-rum pie (Serves 4)

	METRIC	IMPERIAL	AMERICAN
15cm (6 inch) pastry case, cooked	1	1	1
Eggs, separated	2	2	2
Coffee, strong	150ml	¼ pt	⅔ cup
Caster sugar	50g	2 oz	¼ cup
Powdered gelatine	1½ tsp	1½ tsp	1½ tsp
Rum	1 tbsp	1 tbsp	1 tbsp

Blend the egg yolks and coffee in a double saucepan until thickened. Add the sugar. Dissolve the gelatine in 1½ tablespoons hot water, and add to the egg and coffee mixture. Stir in the rum and cool. Beat the egg whites until stiff, fold into the mixture when nearly set. Pour into the pastry case, chill until set.

To freeze Place the pie on a cardboard or foil pie plate, and cover it with another, making sure that it does not touch the surface of the filling. Seal, overwrap, label and freeze. *Storage limit* 2 months.

Thawing Covered, in refrigerator for 4 or more hours. Serve cold.

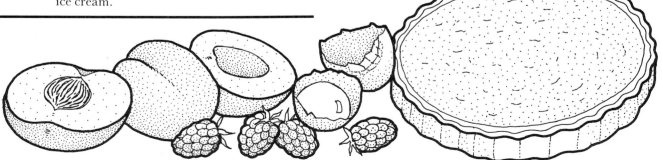

Orange-pear pie (Serves 6)

	METRIC	IMPERIAL	AMERICAN
Ripe pears, peeled, cored and halved	6	6	6
Oranges	2	2	2
Golden syrup	2 tbsp	2 tbsp	2 tbsp
Semolina	2 tbsp	2 tbsp	2 tbsp
Pastry to make 2 × 20cm (8 inch) rounds, using approx. 350g/12 oz /3 cups flour			

Reserve 5 pear halves, and chop the rest fairly finely. Grate the rind of the oranges, remove all the pith, then cut the orange flesh into small chunks. Put all the ingredients, except the pastry, into a pan, cover and cook slowly for about 5 minutes, until thickened. Remove the pan from the heat.

Divide the pastry in half, lining a flan tin with one half. Spoon the cooled fruit mixture over the pastry base, and arrange the 5 pear halves on top. Moistening the pastry edge with water, put on the pastry lid and press or pinch the edges together. Trim the edge, and use trimmings for decoration.

Bake in the centre of a preheated moderately hot oven (190°C, 375°F, Gas Mark 5) for 35–40 minutes until golden.

Cooking time 1 hour

To freeze Cool, remove from flan tin (unless you have used a foil tin in which case it can be frozen in it), put the pie on a cardboard round of the same size. Wrap, seal, label and freeze. *Storage limit* 2 months.

Thawing Overnight in the refrigerator, reheat in a cool oven for 20–30 minutes before serving, or serve cold.

Traditional bread pudding (Serves 8)

	METRIC	IMPERIAL	AMERICAN
Stale bread	300 g	10 oz	10 oz
Milk	150ml	¼ pt	⅔ cup
Water	150ml	¼ pt	⅔ cup
Margarine	50g	2 oz	¼ cup
Jam	50g	2 oz	¼ cup
Mixed dried fruit	100g	4 oz	¼ cup
Mixed spice	2 tsp	2 tsp	2 tsp
Sugar	65g	2½ oz	5 tbsp
Eggs	2	2	2

Cut the bread into small cubes. Heat the milk, water, margarine and jam, stirring, until simmering. Pour over the bread cubes. Beat the mixture with a fork or wooden spoon for a few minutes until the consistency of a soft paste is reached. Stir in the fruit, spice and 50g (2 oz/ ¼ cup) of the sugar, then beat in the eggs. Spoon into a well greased square tin, spreading it evenly. Bake in a preheated moderate oven (180°C, 350°F, Gas Mark 4) for about 45 minutes. Sprinkle the top with the remaining sugar and bake for a further 15 minutes. Tastes best if eaten just a little warm.

Cooking time 1¼ hours

To freeze Cool, wrap and overwrap. Seal, label and freeze. *Storage limit* 3 months.

Thawing Overnight at room temperature; serve cold or reheat in a cool oven.

CAKES

Coffee fruit cake

	METRIC	IMPERIAL	AMERICAN
Flour, self-raising	750g	1½ lb	6 cups
Soft brown sugar	225g	8 oz	1⅓ cups
Ground nutmeg	15g	½ oz	2 tbsp
Ground cloves	1 tbsp	1 tbsp	1 tbsp
Ground cinnamon	15g	½ oz	2 tbsp
Butter	225g	8 oz	1 cup
Golden syrup	100g	4 oz	⅓ cup
Coffee, strong cold	50ml	¼ pt	⅔ cup
Eggs	2	2	2
Milk			
Currants	225g	8 oz	1⅓ cups
Sultanas	225g	8 oz	1⅓ cups

Sift the flour, add the sugar and spices, then rub in the butter. Make a well in the centre. Pour in the syrup, then the coffee. Break in the eggs and beat together well, adding a little milk if the mixture seems dry. Mix in the dried fruit. Place in a well greased tin and bake in a preheated moderate oven (180°C, 350°F, Gas Mark 4) for 1½–2 hours.

Note Makes one 23cm (9 inch) cake or two 18cm (7 inch) cakes.

Cooking time 1½–2 hours
To freeze Cool, wrap in clingfilm or freezer paper. Seal, label and freeze. *Storage limit* 4 months.
Thawing At room temperature, still wrapped, for 3–3½ hours.

Victoria sandwich

	METRIC	IMPERIAL	AMERICAN
Eggs, separated	3	3	3
Caster sugar	100g	4 oz	½ cup
Butter or margarine, melted	50g	2 oz	¼ cup
Flour, self-raising	175g	6 oz	1½ cups
Pinch salt			
Milk			
Jam			

Beat the egg yolks and sugar together until thick and creamy. Add the melted butter or margarine. Sift the flour with the salt and stir lightly into the mixture. Add sufficient milk until the mixture will drop from the spoon.

Whisk the egg whites until stiff and fold into mixture as lightly as possible. Pour into a greased 20cm (8 inch) sandwich tin. Bake in a preheated moderate oven (180°C, 350°F, Gas Mark 4) for about 20 minutes. Cool, cut in half widthways, spread with jam or jam and cream and sandwich together.

Cooking time 35 minutes
To freeze Best frozen uncut, wrap in clingfilm or freezer paper. Seal, label and freeze. *Storage limit* 4 months.
Thawing At room temperature, still wrapped, for 2–2½ hours.

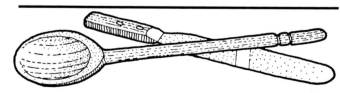

Fairings

	METRIC	IMPERIAL	AMERICAN
Butter or margarine	100g	4 oz	½ cup
Brown sugar	50g	2 oz	⅓ cup
Flour, plain	450g	1 lb	4 cups
Ground ginger	15g	½ oz	2 tbsp
Ground cinnamon	½ tsp	½ tsp	½ tsp
Honey, clear	2 tbsp	2 tbsp	2 tbsp

Cream the butter and sugar together. Add the remaining dry ingredients and warmed honey. Knead into a thick smooth paste, adding a little more honey if necessary to keep the dough from cracking.

Roll out thinly, and cut into gingerbread men or animal shapes. Place on a greased baking sheet and bake in a preheated moderate oven (180°C, 350°F, Gas Mark 4) for about 15 minutes, taking care that they do not scorch. Decorate with icing when quite cold.

Cooking time 30 minutes

To freeze These biscuits soften with freezing, but will crisp up again in a cool oven. Freeze in rigid container. The biscuit dough, shaped or unshaped, can be frozen. Freeze in a polythene bag. Seal, tie, label and freeze. *Storage limit* 4 months.

Thawing At room temperature, unwrapped, for ½–1 hour.

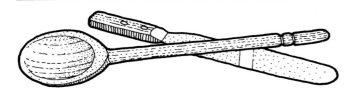

Celebration cake

	METRIC	IMPERIAL	AMERICAN
Butter	350g	12 oz	1½ cups
Caster sugar	350g	12 oz	1½ cups
Grated rind and juice of 1 lemon			
Eggs	8	8	8
Flour, self-raising	450g	1 lb	4 cups
Raisins	225g	8 oz	1⅓ cups
Candied peel	75g	3 oz	½ cup
Almonds, chopped	50g	2 oz	½ cup
Milk			
Glacé icing			
To decorate:			
glacé cherries			
angelica			

Cream the butter and sugar together until light and fluffy. Add the lemon rind and juice, then beat in the eggs, one at a time. Add the sifted flour, raisins, peel and almonds. Mix well, adding a little milk if the mixture seems too dry. Place in a 23cm (9 inch) cake tin lined with greased greaseproof paper and bake in a moderately hot oven (200°C, 400°F, Gas Mark 6) for about 1½ hours.

Ice when quite cold, using glacé or any other icing you prefer. Decorate with cherries and angelica in little flower patterns.

Note If used, American boiled frosting cannot be frozen.

Cooking time About 1½ hours

To freeze Either iced or uniced, wrap in clingfilm and overwrap. Seal, label and freeze. *Storage limit* 4 months.

Thawing At room temperature, unwrapped, for 3–4 hours.

Index

Numbers in italics refer to illustrations